Parenting with Awareness

IN GRATITUDE

This book is written with loving gratitude to my two amazing boys, Ben, and Jake, who chose me to be blessed by the opportunity to grow from their challenges and be honored by their unconditional love. With great appreciation for their father, David, who gave them his best attributes and who stood aside, with grace, to allow me to discover a separate path. To my husband, Steve, whose unconditional love encourages my creative spirit. To my mother who always encouraged my dreams. To my dad who role modeled the courage and determination for me to realize them. To my sister, Ellen, who is always willing to listen without judgment. Lastly, I am grateful to the numerous children and families who allowed me to touch their lives and in the process teach me about the many mysteries of the parent-child relationship.

Parenting with Awareness

Enlightening Our Children and Ourselves
Through Creative Hands-On Activities and
Guided Conversations

MARCIE SCHWARTZ

ORIGINS

Thank you for opening this book. I honor your curiosity to explore new ideas about how to experience life and your role as a parent. This book is written with infinite love for all children and an enormous amount of respect for the challenging, powerful task you have undertaken as a parent. It is written from a place of honesty, humility, hindsight and gratitude for the life experiences I was offered as a teacher and mother over the past three decades. Some were devastating, others a blessing, but all were necessary to propel me forward in my journey of learning. These life experiences challenged my thinking about how the universe works and why, which led me down a path of exploration and discovery. What I discovered is that the universe provides for us in so many amazing ways that I wish I knew about as a young mother setting out on my parenting adventure. Therefore, I want to share them with you to help you nurture and grow our next generation.

As much as possible, I have stayed away from the term *spiritual* with deliberate intent. I hope that you will open yourself up to these ideas without being afraid of compromising your adherence to any specific religious affiliation. All of these ideas are available to everyone. They are not meant to serve any one race or religious denomination. They are meant to challenge old rigid beliefs of how the universe works with and for us. In her book, *How To Live a Prosperous Life,* Catherine Ponder wrote;

"The rich substance of the universe is yours to do with as you wish. Why settle for so little in life when you can have so much, just by daring you to be different in your thinking."

Most of these "New Age" ideas I will present to you have their roots in ancient philosophies and sacred wisdom such as Bible scripture, the mystical teachings of Kabbalah, ancient Eastern philosophies derived from Buddhism and the Toltec knowledge explained to us by Miguel Ruiz in his book *The Four Agreements.* Throughout history, the wisdom of these many teachings was shrouded in secrecy. It was feared that the information was too powerful for the "common man" and that if it fell into the wrong hands, catastrophic consequences would result.

Although derived from ancient teachings, these ideas are relatively new in making their way into our current culture and consciousness, thus deemed "New Age." So why now? Some believe that as the universe moved into the age of Aquarius which began around the year 2000, a universal shift in energy occurred that allowed our minds to open up to the possibility of absorbing this wisdom. This new energy shift is influencing our consciousness away from self-centered thinking to include a more global mentality. As many will agree, this change in how we think and act cannot happen soon enough.

Throughout history, our most famous scientists were first thought to be crazy. Often they were condemned, punished, banned or even put to death for their ideology. One of the most influential of these scientists was Galileo Galilei, commonly known as Galileo. He was an Italian physicist, astronomer and mathematician who lived between 1564 and 1642. He challenged the ideology of the time that the Earth was the center of the universe. Instead he preached Copernicanism - the belief that the earth revolved around the sun. Today we respect Galileo's findings as fact. However, in his time, he was condemned by the church for his views as being contrary to scripture and was tried during the Roman Inquisition. He was found guilty and sentenced to house arrest for the remainder of his life. Galileo wrote, "All truths are easy to understand once they are discovered; the point is to discover them." Discovering them takes an open mind.

As science is making progress in proving some of these New Age notions to be measurable facts, what once has been thought to be magic, mysticism and sacrilege is now becoming acceptable as part of the norm. Two hundred years ago German philosopher Arthur Schopenhauer wrote, "All truth goes through three stages: first it is ridiculed, then it is violently opposed, finally it is widely accepted as self evident."

Because parenting is a long, difficult task, my theory, as a mother, has always been to accept any help I was offered. I have also found it wise to be open to trying things in a new or different way especially if the old way is not working. I hope that by offering you new ideas and ways to approach parenting issues, you will be inspired to challenge your thinking and bring this "new age" awareness into your life and parenting practices.

Being a teacher has offered me the precious opportunity to experience life through the eyes, rhythm and open hearts of thousands of children. I have seen, and appreciate, how every child is truly unique offering her own challenges and joys. Teaching in my parent-child program for the last fourteen years has also offered me the unique setting to observe the beautiful dance that occurs between children and their mothers, leaving me with many enjoyable stories to share with you.

Over the past thirty years, I have been involved with amazing parents who have demonstrated patience, compassion and sacrifice for their children. I have also witnessed many good people with tremendous love for their children, and even with the best intentions, parent so poorly that one might wonder why they ever had children.

One such incident occurred back in the 1980's, when I owned a large daycare center in an affluent suburb of Boston. One night, a half-hour after closing time, one little boy still remained. After numerous attempts at trying to reach his parents through their contact numbers, (remember cell phones didn't exist back then), the teacher on duty had no choice but to follow our protocol. She posted a note detailing the child's whereabouts on the front door of the center and then brought the child to her home and fed him dinner with her own family. It was nearly 8pm before the teacher got a phone call from the frantic father of the boy. Apparently, this professional couple was so preoccupied with their own agendas they each thought the other parent had picked up the child. Once home, they were so involved in the hectic activities of preparing dinner that no one even noticed the child wasn't in the house until the family sat down to eat and he wasn't at the table!

You may be experiencing a sense of disbelief or horror as I did when I initially learned about this situation. Or, perhaps you are judging this family as neglectful and undeserving to be parents. These presumptions will persist until you make your first mothering mistake that compromises your child's best interest. Be prepared. As much as you love your children, you will make mistakes. Then, you'll take a look at yourself in disbelief and ask; "How did I let that happen?" Fortunately, most children survive the humanness of which we parents are so unforgiving of ourselves. However, in that moment, you will be forced to question your priorities of what is truly important to you.

As a teacher, my expertise has come from objective observation of thousands of unique children navigating their personal journeys. Teaching allows an emotional freedom that motherhood doesn't offer. As a mother, my expertise is rooted in humility from the many mistakes I made that only with the grace of God, my two boys and three stepchildren survived. It is my hope that in sharing some of these with you, you will have the foresight to act differently. Many times, like busy families I was preoccupied with my own agenda. Trying to accomplish one more thing in an already too-full schedule, is when I allowed these mistakes to occur.

One of those times was when my son, Ben, who was five at the time, broke his arm. It was a Sunday and I had some organizing to do in my daycare center before the start of the week. I invited a friend to join Ben with the selfish motivation to keep him entertained so I could get my work done without interruptions. I gave the boys free rein to play, unattended, in my gymnastic school, which was adjacent to the daycare center. Ben was swinging on the uneven bars when he accidentally fell. It was the only time in 12 years that I needed to call 911, and it was for my *own* child! This is because I would have never allowed any one else's child to play on the equipment unsupervised. I managed to get through the ride to the hospital with him screaming in pain, two settings of his arm since the first setting was incorrect, and cuddling him until he fell asleep that night, before I threw up from feeling so guilty about failing to keep him safe.

They say that life will continue to offer you situations to learn a lesson until it is mastered. As bad as I felt about my son's fall I obviously didn't learn my lesson, since several years later, when my youngest son, Jake, was two I again was more focused on a task at hand than his safety. At the time, my husband was working in Florida for extended periods of time building a new business. I was in the Boston area running my two schools, taking care of the household responsibilities and trying to be both a mother and father to my two boys. Needless to say, life was busy, stressful and exhausting.

One brilliant afternoon in May, Jake, wearing nothing but his diaper, and I were washing my car. He was reveling in washing the soap off the tires with the hose as my "big boy helper." I heard the dryer buzz announcing the next load of wash could go in. My laundry room was right off the open garage, so I ran in leaving Jake unattended and holding the hose. When I came out about three minutes later, Jake was gone. The sad fact, I have to admit to now, is that I didn't go looking for him. I assumed he went in to the house to find his brother, Ben, since all the doors were wide open. I proceeded to finish washing my car. Then, in a rare moment of peace and quiet, I noticed a strange woman walking up my driveway carrying Jake.

"This baby was playing down by the street!" She screamed at me. "He could have gotten killed in traffic. You should be watching him better." She then handed him over to me as she stomped down my driveway. She was so angry with me that she didn't even acknowledge my gratitude.

Tears streamed out of my eyes as I hugged and kissed him all over his little body. I was so upset I couldn't talk for the rest of the day as visions of all the worst scenarios of what could have happened played through my mind. It was the Thursday before Mother's Day and my husband called to see how our day went. All I could say was that he better not buy me a Mother's Day gift that year because I was the worst mother on the planet and certainly didn't deserve it.

As I write about these events almost twenty years later, I am relieved to say that despite my inexperience, faults and mistakes, my maternal instincts did come through to help my boys successfully navigate their path into adulthood. They are both living out their passions as young adults who are happy, healthy and still enjoying sharing time with me. What more can a mother ask? I am also amazed at how overwhelmed I am with emotion. I can still feel the heartbreak I experienced in those moments so long ago in believing that I let them down. I attribute it to the intense love I have for my boys and the perpetual maternal connection mothers maintain with their children throughout their lives. It demonstrates how all of what we experience with our children changes us forever within our hearts and souls.

"Motherhood: All love begins and ends there."
ROBERT BROWNING

To view Marcie demonstrating the activities
featured in this book please go to

parentingwithawareness.net

TABLE OF CONTENTS

CHAPTER 1

SEEDS OF WISDOM

"What is now proved was once only imagined."
WILLIAM BLAKE

My hope is to plant seeds of wisdom into the minds of mothers that will grow into an awareness to parent in harmony with the universe and utilize all it has to offer us. I, in no way, intend to mitigate the importance of a father's role in the parenting process. It's just that I have never been one. My insights and interpretation of information is definitely from the only perspective I know as a woman in the roles of teacher and mother. I strongly encourage fathers to read this book to bring their paternal interpretation of this information to light because all of these ideas, if they are to work, must become a family philosophy.

The ideas in this book are conveyed with the hope of growing a generation of empowered children who possess the skills, emotions and instincts to successfully navigate their personal journeys into adulthood from a place of unconditional love, joy, prosperity, and fulfillment.

The seed of life is planted within a woman's womb. The miracle of life that then begins to bloom shows us our God-like powers to create something as amazing as a human life. Osho Rajneesh an Indian mystic wrote, "The moment a child is born, the mother is also born. She never existed before - the woman existed, but the mother, never." A mother is something absolutely new. From the miracle of birth, we become mothers and the life-long task of parenting begins. Yes, it is a never-ending process.

As a parent, you are your child's first teacher and life coach. However, your child isn't the only one who is constantly learning and growing from this parent-child relationship. Parenting, no matter how exhausting or frustrating it feels, will require you to rise to the situation and grow and learn through the journey. Parenting is a reciprocal process. Paulo Coelho wrote, "When a teacher helps someone to discover something, the teacher always learns something new too."

As a mother, you are offered a way to test every aspect of who you are and what you stand for over the course of the next twenty-plus years. This school of parenting will test your patience and values, question your decision-making abilities, challenge your strengths, play on your weaknesses and even redefine your relationship with your spouse.

You will constantly have to evolve with each new scenario that is placed in front of you as your child moves along her journey in development. The task of parenting will be the toughest and most rewarding course you have signed on to and it will never be completed. There are those of us who swear that our mothers who have passed are still guiding us from above!

Your children are what you allow them to be. You can offer them unconditional love, nurture their souls and help them grow their dreams. Do this from a place of leadership. Mohandas Gandhi wrote, "Be the change you wish to see in this world." Show them how to live a life of passion, joy and enthusiasm. Fill their days with wonder and awe at the simple things that exist around them.

Society claims parenting is one of the most important jobs you can take on in your lifetime. Ask yourself if you believe this in your heart. Do you trust that you can make a difference or do you believe that only teachers can teach and religious leaders can inspire? Never doubt your role as your child's inspiration. It is always your love that means the most. It is your attention they are willing to sacrifice and work hard for.

Just as there are cycles and continuity to everything on Mother Earth, so are the patterns of parenthood. Thich Nhat Hanh wrote, "If you look deeply into the palm of your hand, you will see your parents and all your generations of your ancestors. All of them are alive in this moment. Each is present in your body. You are the continuation of each of these people." Being a mother has now given you the gift to be a part of this continuation in the rhythm of life.

Your mother birthed you and parented you most likely in similar ways that she was parented. It is part of our programming, conditioning and ancestry. How long after you became a mother did you find yourself sounding and acting like your own mother even though you promised yourself you never would? I can guarantee you that every innuendo, mannerism and belief that you express, especially the ones you hope they forget, will be absorbed and lived out by your children.

As our own mothers age, and we are needed to care for them, the parent child cycle is complete. Our mothers have the joy of experiencing all they have taught you about love, nurturance and patience in the way you care for them. I see the beauty of this mother-child bond in the loving way my husband spoon-feeds his mother who has advanced Alzheimer's.

Your role as a parent is powerful and influential. However, do not feel overwhelmed. The first insight I will reveal to you is a belief based in the idea of reincarnation. It confirms that you are the best parent for each of your children. It claims that before reincarnating into this world, every soul makes an agreement to learn specific life lessons in its next lifetime in order to evolve to a higher level. This means that your children chose you *specifically*. All your attributes, good and bad, including your imperfections and the mistakes you will make, are the exact things that will challenge your children and offer them the experiences to grow and learn in the precise way their soul needs.

For example, if you were lazy in a prior lifetime, maybe one of your life lessons will be to learn the value of hard work. In order to do so, your soul would choose parents who would demand that you work hard. Maybe you would be born into a farming family needing to do many daily chores before heading off to school. Or, perhaps you would choose a set of parents who are never satisfied with the results of your hard work, forcing you to try harder and put out more effort.

So when you think you have totally blown it with your children, remember they have chosen to begin learning their life lessons with you. There will be many other teachers along their journey who will influence and direct them, but you are your child's mentor for life. No matter how many times they fall down, they will always look to you to help them up. It might be hard to grasp your head around the idea that our souls existed before we arrived in human form. But, so many of us were raised to believe in an after life, so why not in a *prior* life?

It is with the hope that through changing our consciousness, we can change the ways we currently exist in this world to create a better situation for our children, ourselves, each other and our planet. You have the amazing opportunity to change the future through your children and what you instill in them.

These ideas will present to you a new way to explore life and approach parenting that will create children who are self-empowered, self-disciplined and self-motivated. Parenting from these principles will allow children to be authentic to their true selves and not try to be someone else's definition of them. They will encourage and respect children to live in their own pace, driven by their own passions and dreams, while not trying to fit a patterned mold of conformity. The ultimate goal of this process is to instill awareness into our next generation that we are all connected. This global consciousness will create compassionate, enlightened adults who collaborate with the concern for the whole rather than selfishly compete at the expense of others. These children will be encouraged to love the process of what they are doing because they are inspired from their passion to realize their dreams.

Brain research has proven that children learn through doing. As *The Course in Miracles* states, "To teach is to demonstrate." The world is very special through the eyes of a child. There is the old saying that you don't know someone until you walk in his or her shoes. By becoming a parent, you have been offered the amazing opportunity to get to wear those child-size shoes one more time. I invite you to step into your child's shoes and stay in them as often as you can. That way, you too, can experience the wonder of discovering these new ideas that are derived from ancient wisdom, through a child's perspective of open-mindedness and enthusiasm.

Our children are crying out for us to do better. They are showing us numerous signs that our way of currently raising children is not working. Less play, more structured activities and parental pressure to excel is creating children who are obese, exhibiting signs of stress, depression and anxiety in unprecedented numbers. Professor David Elkind, in his book *The Hurried Child*, wrote, "The concept of childhood, so vital to the traditional American way of life, is threatened with extinction in the society we have created. Today's child has become the unwilling, unintended victim of overwhelming stress - the stress borne of rapid, bewildering social change and constantly rising expectations." Hard to believe that Elkind wrote those words over twenty-five years ago. You can only imagine how the stress our children are experiencing today has exponentially increased with the advent of new technology, greater academic competition and a floundering economy.

We are all are suffering. Our good intentions and expectations for our children to be better than average result in over-programmed, over-stressed families. Families often run like a business with every minute scheduled and accounted for. The downtime children need to explore their imagination and inner selves is a rarity. However, all of our best creations come from this place of self-discovery and exploration, which is no longer viewed as valuable.

Parents unfortunately have bought into the myth, sold to them by product companies, that they are solely responsible for molding their child's intelligence, talents and ultimate success. This belief creates incredible pressure on parents not to fail. The irony in this belief is that it often demands parents to work extra hours away from their children in order to provide the necessary income to pay for the expensive things they've been told are essential to raising exceptional children. In the book, *No Greater Love*, Mother Teresa wrote, "Everybody today seems to be in such a terrible rush, anxious for greater developments and greater riches and so on, so they have very little time with their parents. Parents have very little time for each other, and in the home begins the disruption of the peace of the world."

Child development experts are all saying the same thing. What children need to develop to their full potential is not the latest educational toys or software. Instead, it is a secure family environment built on unconditional love and unconditional acceptance that will support and challenge their ideas without judgment and nourish their dreams without expectations. This will give them the security and foundation to grow to their full potential. Below is a poem by Grady Sue L. Saxon, educator and author of *How To Raise Children: A Recipe in Plain English* that says this in a sweet way:

Let children be children
While they are young
For in the blink of an eye,
They're grown.
Give them time
To think and ponder
Time to feel and
Look and wonder
Time to question
Why and when
Time to try...
And try again.
Time without the stress
And worry
Of premature demands
And hurry.
Take time to encourage
Love and lead;
And they will create
Explore and succeed!

Teaching children to put away their clothes, to do their homework or to be ready on time may be the parenting tasks that comprise many of your waking moments as a parent. These skills seem rudimentary compared to the invisible qualities of trust, intuition, passion, gratitude, confidence, compassion, courage, morality and patience. These are the essential attributes you should strive to instill in your child that will create a successful, compassionate human being. However, most would agree, this is not an easy task.

Our children are born with open minds and hearts. They are eager to learn all that we have to teach. If we allow them to explore new ideas and assimilate the ones they resonate to, they will become empowered to create their own destiny. They will begin to appreciate their own uniqueness and value that in others. They will see the similarities in the human spirit and build respect for each other's differences. This is founded in the hope of creating the understanding that we are all in search of the same things on this journey called life - unconditional love, happiness and peace.

It takes an honest, secure parent, one who is at peace with themselves, free of ego demands, to be able to love a child into adulthood without conditions. No matter what philosophy or technique you choose, you will most certainly soon realize that there is no recipe for perfect parenting because every relationship between two souls is unique. Each family unit also produces its own energy and is its own entity that constantly changes as the individuals within it change. What works for you and your first child more than likely will not work for your subsequent children. This is why parenting requires a perpetual process of change, transformation and flexibility. There is an old Chinese proverb that says;

I hear- I forget
I see - I remember
I do -I understand

Because children learn through experimentation, this book offers you playful ways to teach your children to embrace life with all of its wonder and potential through hands-on creative, fun activities. These activities will offer the opportunity for self-discovery that will teach children self-awareness and self-reliance so that they understand who they are as unique beings as they interact within the world. These activities will also offer them opportunities to develop skills necessary to face challenges and obstacles they will encounter along the way. Lastly, I hope that by sharing all I learned, I will offer you useful tools that will help you to encourage your children's ideas, believe in their dreams and respect these dreams as their personal road map towards creating the life of which they are so worthy. This book, with all of its ideas, honesty and passion, is my gift to you. Enjoy!

CHAPTER 2

Being Authentic Honoring our True Selves

"The authentic self is the soul made visible."
SARAH BAN BREATHNACH

Knowing and honoring your true self is an essential first step in creating a strong foundation from which to develop your parenting skills. A parent who has a strong sense of identity, a clear understanding of her personal values and a realistic vision of goals will be able to be authentic in her parenting practices. As the Greek philosopher Plato said to his followers, "Know thyself."

Children have a sixth sense about knowing what is real or not. They will know if you truly believe in what you say and do. How many of our parents joked by saying, "Do as I say, and not as I do?" not realizing that their hypocrisy created our distrust in them and everything they stood for. Remember little eyes are always watching. As Ralph Waldo Emerson wrote, "What you do speaks so loudly that I cannot hear what you say." Building on a foundation of authenticity of who you are will allow you to build a consistent, predictable relationship with your children that will foster their true selves to bloom into self assured, happy and peaceful adults.

In 1997, Don Miguel Ruiz introduced to the world his book *The Four Agreements*. It is a little book with a great deal of wisdom and insight about how to live life as your authentic self in happiness and love. The ideas he conveys are derived from the Toltec people who lived at Teotihuacan, the ancient city of pyramids outside Mexico City. The agreements are seemingly simple but take constant practice and discipline to live by. The four agreements, according to Ruiz, are:

1. Be impeccable with your word.
2. Don't take anything personally.
3. Don't make assumptions.
4. Always do your best.

If you take a minute to just sit and contemplate these four agreements you will begin to realize the truth behind this simple wisdom. You might also realize that they are not so easy to live by. So often we find our lives in turmoil because we have mistakenly taken something personally, resulting in unnecessary anger and strained relationships, when in actuality the issue we are angry about had nothing to do with us. Have you ever gossiped or assumed something about another, only later to find out what you believed to be true was wrong? How often have you blamed another for your failures, when in actuality you didn't give your maximum effort?

I have woven Ruiz's four agreements throughout this book to serve as an ideology from which to develop your parenting principles. I encourage you to introduce these agreements to your children so they can serve as a strong foundation from which they can grow. These ideas will take on different meanings and understanding as your children mature. A preschooler can understand the difference between a good or bad word. A six-year-old will be able to comprehend whether she is telling the truth or not. A teenager can understand the concept of gossip. All are aspects of being impeccable with our word.

A quick synopsis of the philosophy behind the four agreements is as follows: According to Ruiz, we all go through a process of "domestication" as children. This is where we learn the appropriate rules and beliefs of our society. Ruiz says that we all want positive attention and it is the fear of losing this attention that keeps us acting in ways that go against who we believe we truly are. Many of us can relate. The fear of disappointing our parents may have been enough to keep us on a track of studying a subject we were not interested in, marrying a person we didn't love or living a lifestyle that didn't mesh with the natural pace of our soul. Ruiz claims that living in disharmony, over time, creates an inner conflict. This conflict causes us to act in ways that go against our authentic selves which, in turn, creates stress.

Byron Katie, author of *Loving What Is,* agrees. She claims that there is "No payoff for the sacrifice. No payoff for seeking what we can never really find from another." That is self-love and self-acceptance. She goes on to say if she had one prayer it would be, "God, spare me from seeking love, approval, or appreciation. Amen." However, the need for attention and parental praise seems to be an inherent human trait that motivates us, visible even in infants. I see it in my six-to-twelve-month old class when babies will repeatedly perform a newly learned skill when provoked in order to gain a positive parental response.

Most of us lived in this conflict of trying to please while ignoring our true desires until adolescence, when we summoned up the courage to defy our parents wishes in an attempt to explore life as our true selves. As teenagers we may have become defiant, missing curfews or skipping school. As college students, maybe we indulged in excessive drinking, experimented with drugs or allowed ourselves to be sexually promiscuous as ways of exploring our individuality. Living out of synchrony with our true selves inhibits us from living in harmony with our soul's desires and discovering our life's purpose. Because of this disconnect, many adults can't identify their intimate dreams or intense passions, never mind live by them.

If you are not living in harmony with your innate desires, then you will constantly need to look outward for happiness. Of course, satisfying oneself from an outward source is a self-defeating game. It's like a pacifier being used to satisfy an infant's hunger. It might be a temporary fix, but it can't quench the real sensation.

Often, after years of frustration, possibly a failed marriage, maybe some physical symptoms of stress beginning to erupt, one usually comes to the realization that this process of living life out of synch with one's self is not working. This disconnect usually leads to some soul searching. It often initiates the beginning of a journey into self-discovery through traditional psychotherapy, a return to religion, or possibly starting a spiritual journey. All of these pursuits are imbued with the hope of finding what was always within us to begin with - our true selves.

The four agreements is about recognizing your authentic self, making the changes to live as your true self and then living by the peace and love you will discover from this process. Aristotle, one of the great Greek philosophers between 384 BC and 322 BC wrote, "Happiness depends upon ourselves."

As adults, so many of us are searching for answers from experts in order to attain happiness, fulfillment and peace. We want to live our lives in joy, but often are so busy, we can't seem to figure out how. We consult therapists, self-help books, websites, shamans and religious guidance hoping something can offer a quick fix. Often, the one place we fail to look is within. The answer to true peace and happiness always lies within you.

As a parent, you may be influenced by the parenting advice from the popular experts of the current trend. There are experts in every aspect of parenting beginning with pregnancy that will offer you advice on how to raise the smartest, best fed, well-mannered child who sleeps through the night, is toilet trained by two, reads before entering preschool and always does what she is told. There are behavior coaches, eating coaches, sleep consultants and tutors all waiting to feed into your parental insecurities. None of them will be able to offer what you already possess-an innate awareness and intimate connection to your child.

This being said, there will be times when you have tapped your gut instincts and innate knowledge and come up with no answers to solve parenting issues at hand. At that point, of course, I encourage you to seek professional help and incorporate that advice into what is acceptable for you and your parenting practices. However, not every expert is the right expert for you. I had this experience early on as a new parent that resulted in an important lesson.

My oldest son, Ben, had a major sleep disorder. He also had twelve ear infections during his first year, so I never could let him cry himself to sleep. This was the acceptable method of getting children to sleep through the night in the 80's. Because I worked full time, this was a huge problem. I was constantly exhausted. This set my husband and I up to establish numerous bad bedtime habits like laying with him in his bed until he fell asleep or letting him sleep in our bed.

By the time he was three, he was still not sleeping through the night and I made an appointment with the esteemed sleep specialist, Dr. Richard Ferber. He had recently written the book *Solve Your Child's Sleep Problems* and was considered to be the expert in the field. I was lucky enough to live outside of Boston, so I was able to see him in person at his Boston Children's Hospital office. I counted the days until our scheduled appointment believing he would hold the magic answer. After much testing he sent us home saying Ben had "Late Phase Disorder" meaning he liked to go to bed late and sleep late. Wow! I knew that. It was an optimal sleep schedule for college but not so great for a preschooler.

He reiterated his theory to let children self-sooth by ignoring their cries for extended time periods. Although I had never been able to let Ben cry it out before, I went home determined to try and do what the expert said. That night was a disaster. Ben was old enough to understand my explanation that we were going to try something new to help him to be able to fall sleep in his own bed. But after putting him to bed, he began to cry and cry and so did I. As much as I wanted it to work, everything about the process went against my gut instincts. The sound of his wails resonated through my every nerve cell. I felt like my heart was being torn apart and that I betrayed his trust. He cried until he threw up and that was the end of us trying the "Ferberizing" method. I know that this method has worked for hundreds of families and I don't mean to minimize its benefits. The pertinent point is that it went against my personal integrity of what felt acceptable to me as a mother.

Soon after that disastrous experiment, I consulted another therapist with the hope of seeking more advice. I was able to take his advice to heart. He said, "You have to honor your own feelings and parent from that place. In that way you will be able to be consistent. From that consistency you will build trust. Not only between you and your child but in yourself to carry out what you believe in." This was extremely valuable advice that I encourage you to remember.

In other words, be honest with yourself about your feelings and beliefs, and from that place create an authentic way of raising your children based on your unique relationship with each one. This may not always be in exact agreement with the experts, but it will be in agreement with what you can honor within yourself. It may have taken me longer to get Ben to sleep in his own bed, but the path was the one I chose. L'ao-Tzu, known as the father of Taoism, wrote, "At the center of your being you have the answer; you know who you are and you know what you want."

Often, we know the truth but are afraid to face the challenges along the way that will ultimately get us to where we need to be. We may perceive ourselves as incompetent or weak, when in reality we have the inner strength to do exactly what our passion guides us to do. We may perceive ourselves as stupid or unqualified to accomplish certain tasks, when in actuality we possess innate wisdom that will guide us in making all big life decisions. We may feel that we are not worthy of unconditional love, but deep down have the instinctive awareness that love is the life force that runs through us all.

Most often, it is our fear that gets in the way of us attempting our dreams. An acronym for fear is "**F**alse **E**xpectations **A**ppearing **R**eal." Fear is just a thought that doesn't exist. It is a mind set concerning the future which hasn't happened yet and over which we have no control. Yet, for many of us we allow this abstract idea to dictate our lives.

Change will only occur when we are ready. I am in no way saying that guides and teachers aren't useful in opening up our awareness to helpful parenting practices. My point is that their message will only be heard when you are open to taking it in because it is in synchrony with what you already know is true for you. It is at that point when change will occur, not *before*.

We want to follow the straight and easy path to happiness but there will always be obstacles along the way. There may be times when we need to move forward, but are afraid to take the first step. Francis Bacon wrote, "We rise to great heights by a winding staircase." There may be numerous signs showing us a clear direction, but we end up overwhelmed and lost. Waking up to all the signs the universe provides is a process. The answers are always visible, but often get hidden behind the busyness of everyday life. How many times have you felt overwhelmed and exhausted by your to-do list? The awareness that your personal peace and how you experience life is always in your power often takes us years to discover. For most of us this insight is a life-long process.

What if we could instill this concept into our children so that they would grow up with the belief that they always hold the power to their own destiny and happiness? The goal is to teach them to look internally for peace and joy and not externally from outward guidance or material reinforcement. This is a difficult task in a culture that is driven by consumerism and external rewards like grades, test scores and who has the biggest, best and most stuff. In order to teach this awareness to your children, you will need to eliminate your own ego from your parenting practices. Instead, choose to parent from a place that will honor your children's uniqueness so they can always remain on their own true path.

Let the beautiful words from *The Prophet* written by Kahlil Gibran guide you. "Your children are not your children. They are the sons and daughters of life's longing for itself. They came through you but not from you and though they are with you yet they belong not to you." This awareness will allow them to grow at their own pace, explore their own dreams and create their own destiny. It is only when we parent from a secure place in our hearts, from our own sense of self, that we can then nurture and respect our children.

Special Me Bottle

What you will need:

- Empty plastic water bottle, label removed
- Colored plastic beads
- Glue gun
- Water to fill the bottle
- Yarn, fabric, permanent markers

Note: Make sure that if you are gluing anything onto the bottle that only you use the glue gun. Glue guns are a wonderful asset for craft making but are extremely hot and dangerous. They are not meant for your children to use!

Before you begin, discuss with your child that each of us is unique and we all have a variety of attributes that make us one of a kind. Give her some examples of a few qualities you use to describe yourself. For example: "I have a great sense of humor." "I am very smart." "I have a quick temper." Discuss how not every aspect of oneself is positive and how we can always strive to improve our weaknesses. You might admit how you are working hard on trying to be more patient. Don't forget to remind her that you love her just the way she is.

Ask her to describe some of her attributes. Explain that each color bead represents one of her traits. Explain that if she thinks she has a lot of a specific trait then she can add in several of the same color. For example, if she thought she was very smart, and chose yellow to represent her intellect, then she might want to place five yellow beads into the bottle. (You might want to write down the attributes she chooses to describe herself, along with the quantity of beads, so you can remember later how she described herself. This will offer you some interesting insights.)

When she is finished placing all of the beads she chose to describe herself into the plastic bottle, fill the bottle with water. Heat up your glue gun. Place the cap onto the bottle and screw it closed, half way. Squeeze a small amount of glue around the top of the bottle, below the cap, and then continue to screw the cap tight. This will force the glue under the cap. Once the cap is tight, squeeze another ring of glue at the bottom of the cap. Wipe off any excess glue. Be extremely careful because the glue will be hot.

Once the bottle is sealed, you can shake it up and see how all the colored beads-the many parts of her-interact to make the one unique person that she is.

If you want to take the activity one step further, you can then let her decorate the outside of the bottle. One idea is to make it look like her. If she has brown hair, you can glue onto the top of the bottle brown yarn. Use the markers to draw features and clothes. You can also glue fabric scraps on to make a colorful outfit. Let her use her imagination. Offer help, but let her make the choices. (If you are gluing anything to the bottle, apply the hot glue to the item first. Let it cool a little before adhering it to the bottle to that the bottle won't melt).

Children are born loving themselves. It is through external criticism, often from us, that they learn to find fault with their bodies and behavior. I once taught an adorable three-year-old who was quite chubby. Her legs exemplified this fact. They resembled the Michelin Tire Man with several roles of pinchable flesh. During our unit about bodies, the children had to make a poster describing their physical characteristics and write down what they liked most about themselves. This little girl wrote, "I love my big legs." All of the staff thought this was hysterically funny since it so went against what society defined as beautiful. At the time my first thought was I wonder if she'll think the same thing when she is an adolescent?

Your conversation while doing this activity together will offer you insight into how your child defines her true self. Unfortunately, as children grow, they become susceptible to the influences of society's judgments about physical appearance and our criticism of their imperfections eroding their self-esteem.

This activity will also push you to look within and be honest about how you define yourself. As adults, we are often more than willing to put ourselves down and be our worst critics. But don't forget to acknowledge all the good that is in you as well. Finally, the goal of this activity is to provide a way for you both of you to honor and respect each other's sense of self and a fun way to grow closer together

All-About-Me Mobile

What you will need:

- 5x7 inch (or larger) picture of your child
- Colored construction paper or cardstock
- Paper punch
- String, yarn or ribbon
- Scissors
- Ruler
- Markers, pen or colored pencils

This is a creative, inexpensive way to allow your child to express her vision about who she is. Our children are so programmed that we don't often allow them time for inner reflection. The process of getting to know yourself and honoring your individual uniqueness can only happen in time set aside to do so. If we begin to teach our children how to focus within early, it will become a comfortable habit that they will grow up know-ing how to do. This ability to check in with themselves will pro-vide them insight into what is important to them as they grow and make their life choices. This awareness will allow them to live in synchrony with who they truly are.

Ask your child to pick out a favorite picture of herself. En-large it to be at least a 5x7 size. Begin the activity by saying that everyone is unique and special. Discuss how it is easy to see the outside of a person but the important qualities that make a person unique and special are on the inside. Ask her to define some of her "inside" qualities that are not always visible. If she hesitates, then offer her an example of some of your traits. This way you are not influencing her self-perception by stating how you see her. Include non-visible things like, "I like the smell of the rain on the sidewalk" or fears like, "I am afraid of spiders."

Explain that you are going to make a mobile all about her. Find the center top of the photo and punch out a single hole with the paper punch. Cut a small piece of string approximately four inches long and slip it through the hole. Tie it off loosely so you will be able to use this string to hang the mobile from. Along the bottom of the photo, punch holes one-half inch apart. This will give you several holes to work with the mobile.

Measure out strips of the colored paper to be one inch wide by six inches in length. You can adjust this size if you need to. Cut out the strips and punch a hole into both ends of the strip. The strip will be hung vertically from each hole. On each strip have your child write one of her attributes. She can dictate them to you, and you can write them for her if she needs help. Mix up the colored paper so the mobile will be colorful.

Measure several pieces of the same length, approximately six inches, of string or yarn. Slip the string through one of the holes of the photo and then knot it tight. Slip the other end through one of the colored strips of paper and tie it off so that it hangs down approximately three to four inches. Do this all along the bottom of the photo to create a row of equal lengths of colored strips full of her attributes.

Do the same thing to create a second row of attributes. Proceed in the same manner until you have used up all the colored strips on which she has written. If you have an uneven amount of paper strips, then center the rows. For example, you could have a row of five, then four then two.

Once you are done, find a place to hang the mobile. You might suggest a place where it can blow in the breeze like in front of a window in her bedroom. You can tell her that the breeze represents the many things that will influence her as she grows. Remind her that changing and being flexible is an important part of growing but that she should only change if it feels consistent in how she sees herself.

CHAPTER 3

Cultivating a Foundation Built on Unconditional Love

"When they placed you in my arms,
you snuggled right into my heart."

UNKNOWN

Our children are born into unconditional love. How many of you set your first glance upon your baby and knew in that moment that you would do anything for that child? Remember breathing in the scent of her? Being in awe of just her existence? This is the first gift that parenting offers, the experience of unconditional love. Which for many of us, is a new sensation. In the instant that your child was placed into your arms, life offered up new meaning. Love is energy. It is from this unconditional love that you will find the energy and strength to endure the thousands of challenges this child will put you through over your lifetime.

This pure, unconditional love probably lasted until she was placed alongside the other infants in the hospital nursery. Immediately, I am sure you looked at the other babies to make comparisons. Is mine the cutest, the biggest, the one with most hair? As your friends and families came to visit, I am sure they reinforced the many ways that your child was special over the others in the nursery. Within hours, this child was already in competition to be better in some way than her nursery neighbors and the unconditional love slowly began to have expectations attached to it.

I once had a friend who gave birth to her first child at age 28. The child had Down's Syndrome. Immediately, the doctor whisked the baby away to attend to her medical issues. Then he medicated my friend to give her some time to rest prior to telling her the shocking news. Meanwhile, her husband had the responsibility of breaking the news to family and friends. He told me the hardest thing was when his mother said to him, "I can't wait to see my beautiful, perfect granddaughter." And he had to respond with, "Mom, she is not so beautiful and not so perfect." Accepting our children as a gift from God means being able to love them with all of their imperfections.

For most of us, from this genuine unconditional love, grows hope and desire for our children. First and foremost, we pray for them to be healthy and thrive. We want only the best for them and strive to provide opportunities and experiences that will offer them something better than what we had. We dream of them becoming successful defined by our own personal agendas. But, how do you determine that definition of success?

As our children grow and move out into the world, it is only natural to compare them with others. In our competitive society, success is often defined by being better than other people's children in academics, sports or the arts. The quest to be better, driven by our own ego, often limits our unconditional love by placing conditions on it, even if it is at a subconscious level. In my classes, I regularly hear mothers questioning other mothers about her child's developmental accomplishments. "When did she begin to walk?" "How many words does she say?" or "What colors does she know?" All are questions asked with the hidden agenda to see if her child is keeping up or falling behind the others.

Unfortunately, even the youngest of children are in tune with this vibration of expectation that emanates from you. They are also keenly aware of even the slightest disappointment towards them from you, hidden in your voice, body language or actions. Author Tony Morrison wrote that what every child wants to know is, "Do your eyes light up when I enter the room? Did you hear me, and did what I say mean anything to you?" If you look into your own heart, isn't she right? Don't you still look for that confirmation, in some way, from your own parents even now as an adult?

One day, one of my three-year-old students spent an entire free playtime making a colorful picture "for Mommy." It incorporated many colors and layers of wet paint. It was an abstract design but to the little girl it was "Me and my mommy at the park, eating ice cream, while watching a dog." While all the children moved from play area to play area, this little girl was focused and determined to create a masterpiece for her mom.

At the end of the morning when her mother arrived to pick up the little girl, she ran to me asking for her picture that was drying on the counter. She was so excited that she was jumping up and down while she waited for me to get it down. At that point the masterpiece was dry enough to take home. When the little girl presented it to her mother, the mother gave it a quick glance and said, "Why don't we just leave it here? We don't have any more room for it at home." In that instant, the little girl's face dropped. I could feel her disappointment and humility, as she knew her mother had judged it to be not worthy to take home. The silence that filled the air was more than enough to create a permanent scar.

You can only love another as much as you love yourself. You cannot give what you do not possess. If you are always critical of yourself, then chances are you will be the same with your child. Everything we do is the culmination of the energy we bring to it. If you feel unloved and expect your child to fill that void, then you are assigning her a task that she will certainly fail. Loving your child needs to come from a place of fullness rather than emptiness.

Love that requires outside reinforcement is not love. It lasts only as long as the reinforcement is there to support it. Love is reciprocal. That is why when we try to satisfy our craving for love through external gratification such as buying material things, striving to be the best, or achieving accolades, it doesn't work. The satisfaction we seek from these things is finite. They can't love you back. Unconditional love is limitless and unending. It satiates because it is essential for the nourishment of our souls. Marianne Williamson wrote, "Love is to people what water is to plants."

Not only is it important to love your child unconditionally, but it is also important for you to build within her a sense of trust in you that your love is limitless. So often sibling rivalries begin over a parent's attention or love. One child may not feel that they are getting their share of you. Children are masters at creating situations that will rope you in and require you to pick sides. This often is the direct result of you giving your children the wrong message; that love is given as a reward and that your love is something that can be earned as a prize for good grades or good behavior.

Because children's lives are so concrete, it may be hard for them to understand something so vast and invisible as love. One way to explain to them that you always have love for all of them is to give them something concrete to visualize the invisible.

A Love Lesson

What you will need:

- **Several candles of different colors or battery operated candles**

This activity will offer you a way to bring the invisible essence of love into something visible. It is recommended for older children capable of handling a lit candle. You can duplicate this activity for younger children by buying battery operated candles. Instead of lighting the candles with a flame, you can just twist the light on.

Make sure you have a candle for each child and yourself. Let each child pick out the color they like. Explain to them that the different colors represent being different people. Now light your candle and tell them that the flame represents your love. Turn out the lights in the room so that it is dark except for the light of your candle. Only do this last step if it won't scare your children. Younger children may appreciate the lights on and the message will still be able to be seen.

As you light each child's candle, ask the children to describe to you what they see. If you are using the battery candles touch your candle to each child's candle as you twist it on. Explain as you light each candle, your flame doesn't get smaller as you share it with them. Instead, love actually grows as we share it. Have them count how many flames there are now from just the one flame. Explain how each one of them has some of your light (love) and you still have your candle lit as well. This is a great visual way for children to see that something can be shared but not diminished or used up.

Using the same candles (unlit), here is another fun demonstration you can do to carry the idea further. Go into a dark room. Tell your child that once again the flame represents love. Ask them how they feel being in the dark room. Are they scared? Do they feel alone? Now light your candle and show them that once there is light, (love) in the room it feels quite different. Go around and light each one of the children's candles. As you do this, the room will get brighter and brighter. Explain to them that as you share love, the good feeling grows from one person to the next. Ask them how they feel with the room being lit by their candles (love). Do they feel safe? Do they feel connected with each other? Let them give words to what they feel and experience. They might surprise you in their ability to capture the message you are trying to convey.

Family Love Necklaces

What you will need:

- **Colored string**
- **Several types of colored beads**
- **Scissors**

When beginning this project explain to your children that love is the invisible thread that connects all of us, as humans, on this planet. Each one of us is unique, but we all share the need to give and receive love to feel safe, feel happy and live a full life.

Begin by showing your child that the colored string represents the love that each of us has in our hearts. Next, show her the many types of colored beads. Explain that everyone is different and that each bead can represent a person who she loves. You can also begin a discussion about how everyone shows their love in different ways. Ask her how she shows her love to the people she has chosen to place onto her necklace. Talk about how those same people show their love to her. You may have to initiate the conversation by giving her some examples. Maybe Grandma brings her gifts and that is the way she knows how to express her love. Maybe the dog licks her face with his wet tongue. Maybe Daddy reads her bedtime stories.

You can then ask her to pick out a bead that she likes the best. This bead can represent her. Now ask her to think of all the people she loves and ask her to choose a bead to represent each of them. If you have more than one child it will be necessary for you to remind each of them that they have their own thoughts and feelings and that it is fine for them to choose different beads to represent the same person. (Sarah can choose a blue bead to represent you and Matthew an orange one).

Ask her to string the beads together to make a necklace of all the people she loves. You can do the same. You can then wear the necklace or hang it up as a decoration.

CHAPTER 4

The Power of Words

*"In the beginning was the Word, and
the Word was with God. And the Word was God."*
NEW TESTAMENT, GOSPEL OF JOHN 1:1

Our words and our language set us apart from the rest of the animal kingdom. In any relationship, words are extremely important. They are a way to express our ideas and emotions. A saying from the Vedas, ancient text originating in India, claims "Speech is the essence of humanity." All of what humanity thinks and ultimately becomes is determined by the expression of ideas and actions through speech and its derivative, writing. Mahatma Gandhi wrote, "Observe your thoughts, for they become your words. Carefully select your words, for they become your actions. Direct your actions, for they become your habits. Examine your habits, for they will become your character. Improve your character, for it becomes your destiny."

For a young child, words are the building blocks of a sense of self. They create an understanding of a place in the world and how things work. Words can motivate or humiliate. They can inspire or limit us from ever trying. They can build one's self esteem, or make one feel small and insignificant. Most of us can remember the power that words have had on us over the course of our lives. Because despite the childhood rhyme: *"Sticks and stones can break my bones, but words can never hurt me,"* most of us would agree that words can, and do, have lasting, emotional effects. With this in mind, it is important for you to be conscientious in your choice of words. Not only in the words you choose to use about yourself, but especially important in choosing words you use in the presence of your child.

In his book, *Aspire,* Kevin Hall wrote the following about the powerful potential of words: "Words have tremendous power for good or for ill. They can inspire or expire. The choice is ours. We can: Choose to heal or choose to wound. Choose to affirm or choose to reject. Choose to inspire or choose to expire. Choose to appreciate or choose to depreciate. Choose to encourage or choose to discourage. Choose to focus on strengths or choose to focus on weaknesses." Take a minute to think about what types of words you choose to use with and around your child.

Before your child was even born, she was listening to your words through the sound of your voice. Research has shown that fetuses know their own mother's voice because an increase in heart rate and non-nutritive sucking has been documented. It has also been observed that parents adjust their speech patterns when talking to their infants by exaggerating sounds and pitch. Parents also adjust their facial expressions, when talking to their infant, by opening their mouth wider and raising their eyebrows.

Altering one's regular speech pattern to gain the infant's attention is called infant-directed speech, "motherese", "parentese" or more commonly "baby talk." Studies have shown that baby talk is preferred by infants and therefore is more effective in getting their attention. Rima Shore, author of *Rethinking the Brain*, believes that baby talk is an important part of the emotional bonding process between parents and their children that helps infants learn the language. Researchers are also raising the question of whether baby talk actually promotes brain development, influencing emotional expression and behavior later on in life.

It is through your words and the way in which you speak them, that you will begin the lifelong process of interaction and relationship with your child. Most child developmentalists agree, as written in *Einstein Never Used Flashcards,* that the amount and type of language an infant hears has an impact on her development. "It is a fact that language stimulation is one of the best predictors of later vocabulary, reading and mathematical skills."

Some ways to enrich your young child's development through language is through songs, nursery rhymes, and reading aloud. As they begin to converse it is important to engage children in open-ended conversations. All of these activities will help build attachment between you and your child.

As a new mom, choosing your words with your child is easy because she can't talk back, question or disagree. You have all of the power and control in the conversation. Enjoy it while it lasts. Because once your child becomes a preschooler, she will start asking "why" questions. Chances are you may have to answer 20 of them before you have even finished your first morning coffee.

As your child grows, your words will be the tools you will rely on to build the type of relationship you want to create with your child. You will use them to praise, discipline, educate, and love. Psychologist Edward Thorndike, famous for his work on operant conditioning suggests one learns from the consequences of one's behavior. He wrote, "Colors fade, temples crumble, empires fall but wise words endure."

Science has proven that everything in the universe vibrates at its unique frequency. Doreen Virtue Ph.D, famous for her books on the angelic realm, claims this theory of vibration includes words. In her book, *Angel Words*, she documents how she measured the vibrational output of words using a computer program that measured the vibration on a graph. Words evoking a positive emotion like the word "love," produced a large vibration, while words producing a negative emotion like "hate" produced a much smaller, constricted vibration. She claims this is concrete evidence showing us that what we say, and how we choose to say it, has a profound effect not only on our relationships, but also on the type of energy we put out into the environment.

Perhaps, the vibrational energy of words is the underlying reason behind how words effect our behavior even if they are introduced on a subliminal level. An experiment headed up by social psychologist John Bargh asked people to unscramble a set of words to create a sentence. He found that when people were exposed to rude words like stupid they later acted more rudely. If they were exposed to words about the elderly, they walked more slowly and when they were exposed to polite words, they later responded with more patience.

As parents, what you say both directly, indirectly, and even subliminally through your actions, will have a distinct impact on your child's behavior and in defining the type of relationship you want to grow with her. This awareness is important to consider when you are trying to instill change in your child's behavior.

For example, if you are trying to get your child to put her clothes away, you might shout, out of frustration: "How many times have I told you not to leave your clothes on the floor?" Instead, an alternative that would evoke more positive energy and a more likely positive outcome might be to say, "Putting your clothes away will make your room look so clean." Or "Putting your clothes away will make me feel so happy!" Most young children want to please. When she does pick up her clothes, reward her by honoring her behavior and how it affected you. You can say; "You really made my day today! I was in such a bad mood until I saw that you put away your clothes. Thank you for helping me feel so much better." This exchange shows your child, that her behavior is part of a relationship. That what she does effects not only her environment and herself, but also the mood of the people she cares about. The family is a microcosm for the world she will have to learn to navigate. It is a practice arena where she will learn what is acceptable, or not, through your guidance, your example and your choice of words.

If you feel that you need to use your power and threats to control your child's behavior, then the next step is to ask why. Is it because that was how you were raised? So many of our beliefs and behaviors come from habit. This includes our parenting styles. It is familiar, so it is comfortable. Just as you may want to change some "bad" habits of your child, you might need to reflect on the process in which you choose to parent. Instilling change in your child's behavior that is motivated by fear of punishment may produce the immediate results you desire, but in the long run will only create a resentful child. Think back to a time when you were forced to do something out of fear. How did you feel?

Discipline is defined as "the practice of training people to obey rules or a code of behavior, using punishment to correct disobedience." It is the process by which we train animals to respond to specific commands. Discipline and punishment do not change behavior from a place of respect. They teach a trained behavior under specific conditions. Discipline, threats and punishment motivate through fear. It is how many past generations parented their children. From this foundation of fear, children grow up with resentment and bitterness, which can create feelings of distance and alienation towards their parents by the time they reach adolescence.

Instead of the word *discipline*, I suggest you think of the word *motivate*. The word *motivate* means to "stimulate interest in or enthusiasm for doing something." If you want to evoke change, I encourage you to do it by utilizing high vibrating energy. Positive words that resonate with love and encouragement have been shown to vibrate at high levels. Using them to motivate a change in behavior will demonstrate to your child that you respect her. This will model the ability to learn self-respect. Appropriate behavior will come from this flow of mutual love and respect.

A goal for parents is to encourage appropriate behavior by instilling the attributes of self-discipline, self-respect and respect for others. This will assure that your child will behave in a consistent, appropriate manner whether she is around you or not. It is also through example that your child will learn appropriate behavior. She started watching you as soon as she was born for directions for how to interact and behave in the world. One thing is certain: Children will mirror your worst behavior. How many of you have joked to your friends that your child went around all day shouting out *sh--* when she got frustrated? She did this knowing full well that this behavior deemed inappropriate by school and others, was acceptable in your home because it was acted out by you. Children learning to behave in socially acceptable ways need consistency between their observations and your expectations.

Motivating Behavior

Here is another example of how to state things from a positive perspective to motivate the desired behavior. A common source of stress for parents of adolescents is asking their child to be home at a specific time and then waiting to see if their child honors that request. This often results in great anxiety as the pre-determined time grows close and the child hasn't arrived home yet.

Instead of saying, "Don't be late or you'll be grounded," which connotes negative energy and a personal threat, you could say; "I know you'll be on time tonight so I won't have to worry about you." This suggests you have confidence in your child's judgment and your genuine concern for her. It also conveys that you love her because if she doesn't come home on time you'll "be worried." It is asking for the same result: your child respecting her curfew. However the second way uses a positive statement, creating positive energy, while the first way originates from a place of negativity most likely creating resentment towards you.

The following word games bring awareness to your child that the words we choose are important because they affect others and the universe. I have offered a variety of activities to accommodate different ages and developmental levels.

Words in a Bucket

What you will need:

- Paper or cardboard
- Markers
- Scissors
- Small container or a plastic bag
- Piece of felt - they usually come in an 8 1/2 x11 size available at a craft or fabric store
- Similar sized piece of sandpaper
- Clear contact paper for protection
- Sticky back Velcro (optional)

This is an activity that will begin to teach your child about the importance of words she chooses. One thing about words is that they can be categorized. This is a great game because it connects a sensory experience, something tangible to the spoken word.

Begin by explaining to your child that there are both positive and negative words. Positive words create good energy and make everyone feel good. Negative words create negative energy, hurt other people and make them feel bad. You can bring this awareness to your child by telling her that you are trying to use positive words instead of negative words. Have her come up with an example or two to see if she understands the concept. If she is too young to fully grasp the idea of negative and positive, you can label words as good and bad. You can also label them by how they make you feel such as happy or sad, scared or excited.

Measure across the top of the paper every two inches. Do the same at the bottom and draw a line between the top and bottom markings. This will give you four columns. Down each vertical side measure one-inch increments and connect those markings. This will create a grid of rectangles approximately one inch by two inches. Write a "good" or "bad" word into each rectangle and cut it out separately. Make sure you have equal number of good and bad words. You and your child can choose words together if she is old enough. This is also a good way to expand her vocabulary. Explain to your child that "good words" are words that create love and happy feelings. Bad words are words of anger that generate bad and sad feelings. You can also explain that negative words that discourage or instill fear in us are words that make you feel dark while words that are full of love and inspiration make you feel light. Give her a couple of examples and let her offer her own ideas.

Place the words into a small container or bowl. Make sure you use the same color markers when writing the words so your child won't pick up on the visual clues of the color. Children are quite perceptive and if you write out all the good words in red, and all the bad words in black, they might cue in to the colors to play the game rather than focusing on the context of the word.

If you are using Velcro, you will need only the rough side on the back of the positive words since this will adhere to the felt easily. For the negative words, you will need to place Velcro on both the sandpaper and the back of the negative word. Make sure you use both the smooth and rough Velcro so they will match up.

For children who cannot read, it will be necessary for you to read the words to them. If your child doesn't know the meaning of a word, you can act out the feeling it creates or show the facial expression it may evoke. This will help your child associate the emotion with the word.

Have your child place the kind words onto the felt and the hurtful words onto the sandpaper. Follow up the game with a discussion of how it feels when someone uses a bad word against you or around you? How do nice words make you feel? How does it make you feel when you use bad words against yourself or someone else?

You can then make a pact with your child that you will both try to use positive words and that you will both remind each other if the other is using a negative word. Children love to teach and I am sure you will give her more than one opportunity to "mind your words." Below is a poem that you can read to your child to reinforce the effects of words on others:

> *If I thought that a word of mine*
> *Perhaps unkind and untrue,*
> *Would leave its trace on a loved one's face,*
> *I'd never speak it --*
> *Would you?*
> *If I thought that a smile of mine*

Might linger the whole day through
And lighten some heart with a heavier part,
I'd not withhold it --
Would you?

(Anonymous)

Motivating Sentences

What you will need:

- **Variety of colored paper or different colored pens or markers**
- **Scissors**
- **Clear contact**

For older children, you may try to create a game based on the findings of the research mentioned above. Remember that words shown to subjects, even at a subliminal level, had an effect on how people later behaved. Think up a few short sentences ahead of time that express motivating ideas using positive words. Write each sentence in a different color marker or on a different color of paper. Then cut out each word separately and laminate it. Place all of the words into a small bowl or bucket and let your child try to make a meaningful sentence by sequencing the words into the correct order.

If you are really clever, you may try to think of sentences that motivate a given behavior you are trying to instill. Otherwise just write sentences that instill in you a happy, joyful feeling.

For example:

Laughing makes me feel happy.
Helping others is the right thing to do.

I love to sing out loud.
Good manners make others feel appreciated.

These are just a few suggestions. See if you can create personal sentences that will resonate specifically to your child's likes and temperament. Then observe if she is in a better mood after playing the game and throughout the day. Even if your experiment doesn't get the exact results you were looking for, you will have practiced reading, sequencing and fine motor skills while having a lot of fun together.

Charades-Style Words

For older children, you can expand on the emotional content of words by acting them out. Begin by placing a variety of "good" or "positive" words and "bad" or "negative" words into a bucket or bowl. Have your child pull out a word and act out how it makes her feel. You can then try to guess the word. For example, you might write out the word "stupid," and when you pull it out you might hang your head in shame or embarrassment. You might want to write the word "creative" which you could act out by pretending to draw an imaginary picture in the air with a big smile on your face.

Helpful Hint

If you are taking the time to make a game for your child, I suggest going the extra mile and protecting it so it will last. To make these games last, laminate the words in clear contact paper. Clear contact is inexpensive. It comes in a roll that would be enough to cover several projects. You can buy this at a supermarket, hardware or craft store. You can also professionally laminate your game at a local office supply or copying location. If you are laminating it yourself with the clear contact paper begin by cutting each word out separately prior to laying it onto the contact paper. It is important to leave 1/4 of an inch between each word in order to maintain the seal. Pull out enough contact to place over several words at once, flip over the contact onto the back of the words and press firmly. This will eliminate any air bubbles. Then cut out each word individually. Start out with just a few words until you get the hang of it. It can be a bit tricky to handle if you pull out too much since it easily sticks to itself.

Sound Wordplay

Many words imitate what they represent such as *meow, hiss* and *moo*. The name for this is onomatopoeia. Have your children think of other words whose sound represents their meaning. You can then ask your children to think of the sound of words they like. My mother once told me that the spoken sound of the words "cellar door" won a magazine competition for being most pleasing to a panel of judges.

The sound, tone and content of words have an impact on our emotions. Ask your child to make a list of the words whose sound makes her feel happy when she hears them. Ask her to try and not think about what the word means, but instead think about what it sounds like. What feelings does it invoke? A great word to start with is the famous 34 letter nonsense word *supercalifragilisticexpialidocious* from the movie "Mary Poppins."

Word Vibration

Understanding the concept for something that exists but, for the most part, is invisible, is important in believing a lot of universal principles I will share with you. Keep in mind that children already believe in a lot of what they can't see. Concepts like magical powers, imaginary friends and the Tooth Fairy are all quite real to them.

As technology advances, scientists are continuing to make progress in measuring the invisible. Everything in the universe has been determined to vibrate at its own intensity. Pythagoras, a sixth-century Greek mathematician and philosopher claimed, "The higher an object's vibration, the more spirit force it contains, hence the more positive in nature." He also proclaimed the opposite to be true. The lower the vibration of an object, the less spirit force it contained, so the object was considered to be more negative.

As I mentioned earlier, Doreen Virtue's book *Angel Words* displays graphs of the vibration emitted from specific words. Her results support Pythagoras' theory. I suggest you read the book. It is a great tool to show your child visually the invisible power of words.

After observing the difference in the graphs between negative and positive words, you can begin a discussion about words. Pose some questions to her about specific words she may use to describe herself, others, her mood or situations. Ask her to imagine what type of graph each word would produce if we had a special word graph machine.

Once again, the beauty of words is that they can be categorized. You can create your own chart or graph system of words based on your personal family values. Some families may consider certain words negative while others not so much.

To begin, explain to your child that there are different types of graphs. You may not have a graph machine like Doreen Virtue, but you can create a bar graph to show the varying vibration of words. You can find an example of a bar graph to show her online.

Word Graphing

What you will need:

- **Graph paper**
- **Colored markers or pencils**
- **Ruler**
- **Scissors**
- **Small bowl to pull out the words from**

Begin by asking your child to think of eight words that make her feel happy, excited or to describe something beautiful. These are high vibration words. Allow her to come up with her own choices. Next have her come up with eight words that make her feel sad, scared or describe something not so nice. These are low vibration words. If she is having a difficult time coming up with any words or is confused in categorizing the words, give her one example of each to start the process.

Take an 8 1/2 x 11 piece of paper and fold it over vertically twice. Then, fold it over twice, horizontally. Cut along each of the folds. This will give you 16 equal sized squares. Write one word on each piece of paper and fold it in half so that you cannot see the word. Place each word into a bowl.

If you are using graph paper you can skip to the next step. However, if you are using plain paper you will need to create the framework for your graph. Using your ruler, measure one-inch increments up the long side of the paper. Now do the same across the short side. Draw a straight line between the markings to create a grid. After you create your grid turn the page vertically. This will offer you the option of measuring up 11 blocks. You can place numbers along the left hand side if you want to but it is not necessary.

Next have your child pull a word from the bowl. Ask her to think of a color that this word conjures. Give her an example like the word *happy* makes you think of *yellow.* Using the corresponding color marker or colored pencil, have her color in what she thinks is the height of the vibration of the word she picked. This is subjective of course but it will give you insight into her interpretation of the words. You can take turns or have her continue. Seeing how she interprets certain words will offer you awareness as to what words you might choose to use with her in the future.

When the graph is complete, you should have a great visual to open up a discussion about the power of words and the influence they have on those with whom we talk. Ask her if this has helped her understand the effect that words have on the way we think and feel. Most importantly, ask her if she understands how the power of her words effects the way others think and feel.

Feeling Vibration

Teaching what vibration is to children can be quite exciting. One way to begin to teach your child about vibration is to have her place her hand upon her throat and say words. We all have our first instrument right within each of us and that is our voice. She will feel the natural vibration of her vocal chords resonating with her spoken words. This will be more effective if you sing a song she knows by heart like "Happy Birthday." That way she will feel the different vibrations without thinking of what word she wants to say. Explain to her that singing is an act of vibration so she equates the vibrating sensation to the term.

Throughout this book there will be many references to vibration. Here are a few visual ways to allow your child to see vibration in action.

Watching Pepper Dance

What you will need:

- **Small bowl**
- **Plastic wrap**
- **Rubber band**
- **Pepper**
- **Wooden spoon**
- **Small pot**

Cover the bowl with the plastic wrap. Pull the plastic tight across the top in all directions until it is flat and smooth. Use a rubber band to tightly secure the plastic wrap. Then sprinkle some pepper onto the plastic and make some noise! Hold a pot and spoon near the bowl and hit the bottom of the pot hard. What do you see? Explain that the loud noise you made created a vibration. Explain that the vibration gets transmitted through the air, to the plastic. The plastic vibrates and makes the pepper dance. Wow! You will surely be the hit of the day with this activity.

Rubber bands are also a great way to see vibration. Give your child a rubber band to stretch between her thumb and forefinger. Remind her not to point it at anyone. Explain that it could hurt them, especially their eyes, if it accidentally shot off and hit them. While the rubber band is stretched tight, have her use her fingers on the other hand to pluck the rubber band. What happens? Explain that the rubber band vibrates and that is what makes the sound.

Rubber Band Music (older children)

What you will need:

- **Wooden board, approximately 12 inches x 12 inches**
- **Nails with a large head**
- **Rubber bands of varying lengths**
- **Hammer**
- **Ruler**
- **Pencil or marker**

Some of you might remember a version of this activity when you were a child. Across the top, sides and bottom of the board, measure one-inch increments. Draw a line from top to bottom to the corresponding point and from side to side to create a grid.

Now hammer a nail into the intersection of each line. Make sure they are equal in height. Depending on the age of your child, you can let her hammer the nails. It might be a good idea to start the nail and just let her finish it. Be careful not to hammer the nail all the way down into the board since the rubber band will have to hook onto the nail head!

Once the nails are secure, allow your child to stretch a rubber band between two nails. Explain to her that she can stretch them vertically, horizontally and diagonally. If you need to buy the rubber bands, I would suggest that you look for a variety pack that will offer you different lengths in different colors. This will add a little color and the possibility of creating designs to your board. *Voila!* You have just made an instrument.

Now you can begin to experiment with what happens when you attach different length rubber bands to the nails. Explain to her that she can experiment with stretching a small band over a long distance. How does this effect its vibration? What types of sounds can she make? How does the music vary depending on how tightly the rubber band is stretched? What if she tries to stretch the rubber band on the diagonal? What happens then? What happens if she places two rubber bands on top of each other? These are just a few questions to ponder. I am sure she will come up with her own.

The Ha-Ha Game

What you will need:

- **Two or more people (It will be more effective with several children)**
- **A willingness to be silly**

Have you ever played the Ha - Ha game? This is a game that will surely fill your day with laughter -- guaranteed. It's a great way to connect with your child and feel each other's vibration. Lay down on the floor face up and have your child rest his or her head on your belly while laying perpendicular to you. Tell her you are going to take turns saying "Ha". Each time it is your turn you have to add one more "Ha." She will feel your voice resonating when her head is on your belly. Then you begin by saying, "Ha." Then she says, "Ha, Ha." Then you say, "Ha, Ha, Ha." Continue to take turns saying "Ha," increasing by one each time. After you lose it with laughter because one of you *will,* switch. Rest your head on her stomach and let her start. There is nothing like a good belly laugh. The positive vibrations you both will put out will fill your space with humor, love, and guaranteed fun!

Now that you have experimented with vibration, your child will have a sense of what we will be referring to throughout this book. You can explain that most things vibrate so fast that's why we can't see it.

CHAPTER 5

BEING IMPECCABLE WITH YOUR WORD

*"Use the power of your word in
the direction of truth and love."*

MIGUEL ANGEL RUIZ

The first of Ruiz's four agreements is to "Be impeccable with your word." Teaching this skill to your child will begin with you as a role model. Acknowledging the importance of words is the first step in the process of learning to be impeccable with your word. The word *impeccable* originated from the Latin *impecca-bilis* in the mid 16th century. It comes from in-'not' and *peccare* meaning 'to sin." Therefore, to be impeccable with your word means to speak without sin. It is asking you to speak with the highest standard of propriety. It is asking you to be sinless not only in your spoken word but also in the intent behind your spoken word. It is to speak with honesty, compassion and love. Not with words full of blame, guilt or judgment. It means to speak to others with respect and dignity, the way in which you wish to be spoken to.

It is a hard enough task for us as adults to learn to be im-peccable with our word. How do you begin to teach this skill to your children? First of all, your children have an advantage over you. They have a clean slate. You need to unlearn all the limiting beliefs, and bad habits that you have acquired over your lifetime.

Today, children are lucky to be born into a time of change. It's a time of new awareness and acceptance. Words and concepts like *karma*, *green*, and *connectedness* are relatively new words conveying ideas that are moving into the mainstream of everyday language and awareness. It is from this place of openness that your child will have an opportunity to bloom, grow and realize her full potential with your love and guidance and of course, your words.

The first step in learning to be impeccable with your word is for you to become cognizant of your unspoken thoughts and how you choose to present them. This is a lifelong process of simply being aware of what we say and how we say it. Eliminate all negative self-talk. This is something parents often model without even being aware of it. Be conscientious if you are one who says things like, "I'm so stupid, I lost my keys again." Or "I hate my body. I look like a fat pig in this bathing suit." Ruiz writes in *The Four Agreements,* "How much you love yourself and how you feel about yourself are directly proportionate to the quality and integrity of your word. When you are impeccable with your word, you feel good; you feel happy and at peace." If you model to your child that it's okay to put yourself down, they too will begin to follow suit when they are frustrated or unhappy.

It is imperative that you do not talk negatively about others in front of your children. This is critical because little ears tend to hear everything except for what you want them to hear. You may ask your child to put away her toys ten times and she will play deaf to ignore your requests. But believe me, she will be able to recall something of intrigue you said during a phone conversation to a friend that wasn't even directed to her. If your child hears you say things like, "Your dad is so selfish. All he wants to do is play golf on Saturday instead of being with us." Your child will learn that it is okay to judge and criticize others.

Most importantly, it is imperative to never role model gossip in front of your children. Gossip is defined as "casual or unconstrained conversation or reports about other people typically involving details that are not confirmed as being true." To participate in gossip is to perpetuate lies. If we want to teach our child how to recognize and respect their own truth and always speak the truth, we cannot allow ourselves to get dragged into conversations with our friends based on gossip. Because telling the truth is the most important part of being impeccable with your word, gossip, which is created from misinformation, or lies, is the opposite.

Today, because of the numerous social networking sights on the Web like Facebook, gossip and being into everyone else's business has become part of our daily routines. The danger about the social networking sites is that they allow people a place to anonymously gossip without needing to take personal responsibility for their actions. Teach and role model to your child that it is not okay to talk about someone if they are not present. Otherwise you can never know how your words made them feel.

Being impeccable with your word means not to lie in front of your children. As obvious as this seems, many of us have done it. It may have been dismissed as a "white lie" to get us off the hook for something we didn't want to do. Have you ever said, "I'm sorry but I have plans on Thursday," when you didn't want to volunteer at your child's school? Maybe you lied to your husband when he questioned why dinner wasn't ready and you said, "I didn't have a minute all day to myself" while your child observed you watching TV for an hour on the couch.

It is impossible to teach your child the difference between a good lie and a bad lie. There is no such thing. Teaching your child honesty is essential to them creating harmonious relationships. Practicing honesty in their thoughts, feelings and words is essential in helping them establish self worth, respect for others and living life in an authentic manner.

Muddying the Waters

What you will need:

- **Clear glass**
- **Water to fill the glass**
- **Small bowl of dirt**

This is a great visual of how gossip can poison our thoughts and harm others. Fill the glass with water. Tell your children that the glass of water represents what happens to them or another when they gossip. Begin by saying that you are going to show them how gossip makes people feel. Then, open with a line of "gossip" like "I heard that Mrs. Duggan is getting a divorce." While you are gossiping, take a small spoon of dirt and place it into the water. Show the children how the gossip dirties the water so it no longer is clean and clear.

Next urge your child to relay some gossip and allow her to add a spoonful of dirt. Continue on until everyone has had a turn. Now ask, "Who wants a drink?"

Begin a discussion about how gossiping gives us negative energy that makes us feel dark and dirty. It also affects the other person by hurting her feelings and making them feel sad. Show your child how it is nearly impossible to get rid of the effects of gossip once it has been spoken. (Remind her about the dirt in the water.) Explain that once we put gossip out into the universe, it stays there as negative energy. Even if we can't see it like the dirt, its effects are still there in the way it makes others feel.

Discuss the possible ways they could use to make the water clean and clear again. See what they come up with for ideas. Can they ever get it clean enough to drink it? Then offer the example of pouring the water through a filter, which could represent an apology. Show her that the apology (filter) helped clean the water, but it can never be the same, clear, clean water that it was. Follow up with a conversation that no matter how hard you try to clean away the negative effects of gossip, some effect always stays behind. Because once your words are spoken, the energy they create is let out into the universe and cannot be recaptured.

CHAPTER 6

BEING CONSISTENT WITH YOUR WORDS

"Your words mean nothing to me because your actions spoke the truth."

UNKNOWN

One of the most important things you will need to master as a parent is to be consistent between your words and actions. This demonstrates to your child how to be honest in expressing your feelings. It is also teaching a child about cause and effect which is an essential skill to learn. Most importantly, it is a way of teaching and establishing trust with your child. Your child will learn to trust your words if you are true to them.

It is essential to be clear in your thoughts before you speak. This might mean that you have to pause and think before you yell out a threat, or offer a promise that you may not be able to keep. Children are extremely quick learners when it comes to manipulating us through our feelings. If you threaten with a punishment, then you need to follow through. I have heard dozens of mothers say, "I am counting to three and if you don't pick up your toy or put on your coat, we are going to leave without it." Then the mother counts slowly to three and the child continues to play and ignores her request. Then the mother does nothing. Mom then repeats her threat with, "I'm going to say it one more time." The scenario goes on and on until the child gets bored, and decides she is ready to go. They leave as if the whole exchange never occurred. There is no repercussion or follow through on the mother's part for the lack of cooperation from the child. From these types of interactions, do not be the least bit surprised years later when your child is an adolescent and you threaten, "You can't go out until you finish your homework," and she throws her books down on the table and stomps out of the house, with never a look back.

What the above scenario also teaches your child is that you have so little respect for yourself and your desires being met, that it is okay for her to disrespect you. You not only allowed it to occur, you actually encouraged her lack of respect by affirming your request and accepting her lack of response. Each time she didn't respect your wishes, you allowed yourself to be humiliated. This is way too much power for you to give away to anyone, especially a young child. Once your child knows you can be manipulated and there are no consequences for her lack of cooperation, she will repeat this pattern of testing you until it becomes a way in which you both approach conflict. As a parent, you will experience conflict with your child as soon as she begins to recognize herself as separate from you at around 15-18 months. At that time, the conflict may be as simple as trying to get her to clean up her toys. Later on, it might be about taking her responsibilities seriously and making appropriate life choices.

Parents want to avoid conflict because it often requires a more difficult response from them in the moment. The Chinese word for *crisis* is composed of two characters: One represents *danger* the other represents *opportunity*. These small moments of conflict or crisis are offering you the opportunity to build a trusting relationship with your child. The danger presents itself only if you don't see the opportunity and take the easy road of non-reaction. Each conflict presents an opportunity to learn respect and negotiation which are two essential life skills. In my classroom I have had children who have acted out during our structured circle time. This can mean anything from running wildly around the classroom, pulling toys out from a closed cupboard or screaming in full-blown tantrum style if they don't get a specific toy they want. Some mothers will sit back and do absolutely nothing, allowing the child to disrupt the entire class. Others may attempt to reason with them, a difficult goal to accomplish with a two-year old. This most often results in the child getting what she wants after the reasoning fails. Thus, giving in to her demands.

Some mothers threaten to leave. This is meant as a warning for the child to change his or her behavior since the child usually wants to stay despite his or her lack of cooperation. However, after several attempts of ineffective intervention and threats to leave, only a handful of mothers ever do. Leaving requires carrying a kicking and screaming child out of the building with the mother aware that all eyes are on her. What she isn't aware of is that most mothers are looking on, not in mockery, but in admiration because they wish they had the strength to stand within their power and do exactly what she just did.

Children's desires can be enduring and their energy endless when they want something they can't have. Most can wear an adult down in a matter of minutes. Your resolve to be consistent in these testing situations, which I guarantee you will repeat themselves throughout your parenting, is key for you to maintain your child's respect and trust.

For the young child, you need to react in the moment to a specific behavior that will allow her to make a connection between the cause (her behavior) and the effect (your response).

The time lapse can lengthen, as children get older, and as they learn more about the principle of karma, to be discussed later.

Patterns of behavior become habits which can become a way of interacting within our world. Following through on everything you say may be harder to endure in the moment but will save you a lot of frustration, arguing and resentment in the long run. If you do not follow through, the subliminal message your child receives is "I cannot trust what my mom says." If a child can't trust your words regarding the small promises, good or bad, how can she ever come to you for advice or count on you for future promises? Saying what you mean and acting accordingly is all about teaching your child that she can trust you.

As a parent, we often use our words with the intention to motivate our children to try harder or do better. It's important to not use words of judgment against your child or her efforts even if you are not happy with her performance. You may think your child isn't doing her best but maybe in that moment she really is giving it all she has.

Your child's sense of confidence and place in the world is going to be directly effected by how she is motivated by you. Saying things like, "You are lazy, you never try your hardest," are words of anger and disappointment. When we use angry or hurtful words against another, even if it we justify our tactics by our so-called good intention to motivate, it is coming from a negative place within ourselves. It is your ego's need for your child to be better than who she is or at what she is doing. Words of judgment do not motivate. They limit and condemn a child for failing to live up to your arbitrary expectations.

Lastly, do not talk about other nations or races with bigotry or hatred. Children come into the world with love in their hearts for all. Maya Angelou wrote, "We all should know that diversity makes for a rich tapestry, and we must understand that all the threads of the tapestry are equal in value no matter what their

CHAPTER 7

Trusting Your Parental Intuition

"There is no instinct like that of the heart."
LORD BYRON

The word *intuition* means "to perceive directly without reasoning." The biological and emotional connection you have with your child offers you an innate intuition stronger than you can experience with any other human being. Often, mothers know things about their child's health or behavior long before a diagnosis is uncovered.

Years ago, my mother-in-law told the story of how she had a dream while traveling in Europe about one of her daughter's cheeks inflating and deflating like a balloon. She said she awoke with a panicky feeling in the pit of her stomach knowing she immediately had to call home. Upon calling she learned that her daughter had contracted the measles.

I encourage you to trust your intuition and cultivate it. Tuning into your senses and listening to your gut feelings will enable you to make decisions based from your personal truth and not from external pressures. "Our intuition usually makes itself known to us in a flash, and often has a physical component - a flutter in our stomachs, sweaty palms, or a chill. When we use this information to help us navigate a situation, we always benefit."(Daily Om, 2010)

Tuning in to your intuition requires you to be still and silent long enough to hear its subtle cues. If you are always rushing, living in chaos and bombarded by noise, then you won't be able to recognize the signs that may be obvious. It is my belief that it is through your intuition that God speaks to you. You just need to believe enough in yourself to listen. Through practice and positive experiences, you will begin to trust this gift within you. Once you begin to trust your intuition, it will offer you insight and discovery into your child that may otherwise have gone unnoticed.

Trusting your intuition enough to act on it can prevent a potentially dangerous or hurtful situation. This is something I know all too well because I didn't have the courage to trust what I intuitively knew to be wrong. It resulted in the most painful experience as a mother that I have had to endure. The lack of trusting my own intuition, and having the confidence to react to it, resulted in a chain of life-altering events that compromised the safety of my son Ben.

This is an extremely personal story I share with you in the hope that when you are faced with a situation, regarding your child's desires, that opposes your maternal instincts, you will have the confidence to trust your gut feeling even if it means disappointing your child in the moment. Children will get over anger. They will resolve conflicts with you. But they may not survive a life-threatening situation that you may have been able to prevent if only you had the faith to act on your intuition.

The situation involved an 18-year-old man I will call Andrew, whom I hired to install our computer. He was extremely bright and was more than willing to return to our home with any computer problems and questions I had. As a single mother who was not very technically inclined, he was a gift. Looking back, we did have an unusual amount of problems for a new computer that required his return several times.

With each visit, he would bring a computer game for my son Ben who was twelve at the time. He began to spend time playing these games with him. My instinct told me that something wasn't right with an 18-year-old wanting to spend time with a 12-year-old. However, Ben had been feeling despondent about our recent move and his spirits lifted when Andrew arrived. I ignored my unease and let the friendship continue. I allowed my son's immediate happiness to outweigh my better judgment. It was easier in the moment not to fight him than to stand up for what my inner guidance was trying to tell me.

This friendship blossomed under my cautiously watchful eye over the course of the next two years. Despite my unease, I was unaware of any unusual activity. That is until one weekend, while I was away, my ex-husband called me in a panic to report that Ben and Andrew were found by the police in a state park together at 4 am! According to Ben, they were waiting for the stores to open so they could be the first in line to purchase the latest electronic devise they both wanted.

At that point all of my worst fears began flashing through my mind. I was swarming in guilt because I knew something wasn't right from the beginning and I didn't have the courage to stop it long ago. Ben was interviewed by the police and appeared unscathed. In a typical teenage fashion he was furiously angry with the police and me. He couldn't understand why we all were making such a big deal over nothing.

As is so often the case in parenting when you wait too long to respond, you will usually overreact in full force. I told Ben that he could no longer see or communicate with Andrew. I also summoned Andrew to my home and told him face to face that he was never to contact my son, in any way, or I would call the police. Ben thought I was horrible and unfair. After all, it was true, up until that point Andrew had never attempted to hurt him. Perpetrators are the best at diminishing our intuition because they are very cunning and patient. Most perpetrators take years to ingratiate themselves into their victim's life, slowly building trust long before they attempt to hurt.

I wish the story could end there and I could tell you that Ben and Andrew listened to me, the all-powerful and respected mother, but it was only the beginning. Late one Friday afternoon I received a call from Ben demanding that I come get him right away behind the public library. Once again my intuition clicked in. I sensed an unusual panic and urgency in his voice. For that reason, without question, I immediately went to get him.

The first thing I noticed as he walked towards me, was that he wasn't carrying his backpack and that his cheeks were bright red. As he approached the car, he started to tell me that Andrew had tried to *shoot* him!

Ben confessed that he met Andrew because Andrew promised to give him the computer game he wanted. Ben reported that he got into the back seat of Andrew's car. They spoke briefly and Andrew gave him the game. Ben thanked him and said, "See you later dude." As Ben moved to get out of the car Andrew locked the doors with the automatic door locks. He described that Andrew pointed a gun at his head and said, "You are not going anywhere." Despite my son being a third the size of Andrew, he was able to force Andrew's arm aside as he managed to unlock and push open the car door. As Ben fell out onto the ground Andrew fired a shot at him but thankfully missed! Andrew then sped off leaving Ben in the parking lot in shock but unharmed.

As Ben told the story my first reaction was horror and disbelief. The idea of Andrew threatening my son with a gun was beyond my comprehension. Panic filled me with adrenaline and overwhelming nausea. The police were stymied since this type of crime was unheard of in our quiet Boston suburb. They sent out numerous officers and a helicopter to search for Andrew's car, but he was long gone. He drove all the way to Nebraska before he turned himself in two days later.

The legal process was frustratingly inept and did absolutely nothing to protect my son. Because Andrew had no prior record he was released on parole. For the next several years, Andrew continued to torment Ben by stalking him electronically. When it came to computer savviness, Andrew's brilliance allowed him to hack into Ben's email, disable our hard drive and make his presence known to Ben on a regular basis without ever being seen.

Five years, after the attempt on my son's life, Andrew called Ben on his nineteenth birthday and left the message. "How would you like me to blow my head off for your birthday, birthday boy?" It was a Friday and Ben was on his way home from college in Michigan to celebrate his birthday with family and friends.

Immediately when Ben arrived home from the airport, we walked over to the police station situated across from my house. The police spent hours trying to track Andrew's phone number to see if it was a cell phone number or a landline. After spending several hours in the station with no firm information to fall back on, we returned home. The police promised to patrol the area and watch over our comings and goings. The next day, Saturday, was peaceful as if nothing occurred.

On Sunday morning, my two boys were rushing around preparing to leave the house to see their dad before Ben's plane departed. He had a 4 pm flight. He left at 12:15. Minutes after saying goodbye I saw a man of slender build walk into my back yard. You would think I would have recognized him as Andrew but I didn't make the connection because the Andrew I had known was over 300 pounds. I yelled out to my husband that a man just came into our yard and went under our backyard trellis, but I didn't see him leave. My husband didn't make the connection, either, and he went out back to see who it was. I know it seems bizarre that neither of us suspected that this man was Andrew. Nor did we call the police after the prior events of Friday. I truly believe that everything happens for a reason and that the universe was intervening so that the events would unfold just as they needed to do.

As I watched out the back window I observed my husband talking to the man who was hidden from my view underneath the trellis. After a brief conversation, as if in slow motion, I observed my husband slowly turn to walk away when I heard the shot. After five years of agony and torment for Ben and my family, Andrew walked into my back yard, sat down against my basement door and *shot himself in the head*!

In that moment I didn't know if he was dead or had attempted to fire at my husband and was still lurking in my yard. I remember screaming in terror as I called 911. Within minutes our house became a crime scene. The yard wrapped in yellow tape and the street lined with police cars. After several hours of questioning, a dozen officials packed up and left us to decipher the trauma of the days' events.

During the afternoon I managed to call Ben to tell him. He was shocked but ecstatic. His worry was now over. He was free. What he then said to me only confirmed that the universe had managed to protect him from harm throughout this entire process. He said, "Mom, you are not going to believe this, but my flight isn't at 4 pm it's at 7 pm!" This misinformation guaranteed that Ben was safely away from the drama that unfolded at the house. He then said, "I don't even care that I have to wait here three hours. I'm happy to do it." It was in that moment that

Ben was given a new lease on life. For me, as a mother, I could begin the long process to forgive myself for not trusting my intuition and protecting him.

I am grateful everyday that my son is alive, vibrant and thriving. It is by the grace of God that Ben has had the internal strength and character not to allow this event to disrupt his life plans and personal happiness. So often we allow the identity of victim to define us throughout our lives, robbing us of our personal power and limiting our full potential to bloom. Ben has not let this event define him. I am so very proud of his inner strength and attitude.

We can only keep our children safe while they are within our sight and reach, and even then, not always. As soon as we let them out of our controlled environments, they are going to be bombarded with constant challenges that have the potential to compromise their safety. We are no longer living in a predictable world in which we can trust external authority figures and prior ideas about reality to guide us. Children have been raped in the finest schools and our holiest of buildings. They are bullied by peers and challenged to do dangerous activities to earn the respect of their friends.

It is important for them to be taught that what they see or hear may not always be the truth. As in the story above, someone that appears nice can actually be dangerous. This is an extremely difficult concept for any one to accept including adults. Look how hard it has been for church communities to believe that their beloved priests were indeed child molesters. The idea of villains lurking in disguise waiting to prey on innocent children has been conveyed in children's fairytales for centuries like "Hansel and Gretel" and "Little Red Riding Hood." You can use these classics to introduce this idea to your young children. If you do, make sure they are aware of the concept of real and make believe to help avoid nightmares.

Trusting one's intuition is a gift. It potentially can teach children to keep themselves safe in a precarious situation if they are tuned into their inner guidance and innate wisdom. If you begin to train your child to listen to her intuition, while young, then as she grows she will be tuned in to the synchrony of her feelings and her perceptions and know if something does not "feel right."

How can you as a parent teach your child to recognize and trust the message their bodies are trying to tell them through a gut feeling? The human body is amazingly capable of this challenge. We possess the flight or fight instinct when we sense danger with all kinds of bodily sensations. In order for a child to learn how to tune into bodily cues, she must have the opportunity to experience quiet time. Practicing stillness and listening are essential skills required to tap into our innate guidance system.

One way to practice tuning in to one's intuition is to teach children to intuit the true meaning behind someone's spoken words. According to Albert Mehrabian, author of *Silent Messages*, "A listener perceives 55 percent of the meaning of the spoken message through gestures and facial expressions; 38 percent is interpreted through tone of voice, speech rate, rhythm and emphasis; and words transmit approximately 7 percent of the message. In other words, nonverbal cues communicate the bulk of the message." Therefore, it is quite helpful for children to practice observation of body language and listening skills.

A fun way to build listening skills is to practice through word games. Begin with a discussion reminding her what it means to be impeccable with her word as we discussed in Chapter Five. Remind her that it's important to always strive to be honest in our choice of words spreading positive energy out into the universe and to others.

However, you will need to raise the issue that not everyone she meets will be authentic in what they say. Ask her if she has any friends who have ever lied to her or said something different from what they truly felt. Has she? Unfortunately, mixed messages, innuendoes and sarcasm are all forms of speech your child will need to decipher on a regular basis. You can offer her an example. A common one she might have experienced is saying, "I don't care." When a friend asked her, "What do you want to do?" Point out that in reality she did have an opinion and a preference of what she wanted to do.

You can pose other questions such as:

How do you know if a friend really likes you or is just using you for something she wants?
Can you trust someone who promises you something only if you do something in exchange?

These are just two examples of possible situations she may face as she navigates social situations. If she is experiencing any specific incident in her life, try to work that in to the discussion.

Guess What I Mean Listening Game

Begin by saying that you are going to play a game where you have to try to guess if the other person is telling the truth. You will also learn how to feel what their words mean. Explain that you might try to trick her so she needs to listen carefully to not only your words, but also the intention behind your words - *how* you say them. Also explain that she should watch your facial expressions and body language. Draw upon your acting skills to make this fun. If you don't think you have any, then just remember back to your own adolescence and a situation when you easily played a role to put one over on your parents.

Here is an example for her to intuit her friend's true intentions, "I want you to guess if Amy is Sadie's friend or if she just wants to play with her new video game?

Amy: "Hi Sadie. I heard you got the new video game everyone wants."

Sadie: "Yeah, my dad ordered it online months ago so I would be one of the first to have it."

Amy: "Wow! You are so lucky to have such a nice dad. I love your hair. I wish my hair was as pretty as yours."

Sadie; "Thanks."

Amy: "I love your boots, too. That pink is my favorite color. What color is your room?"

Sadie: "Purple and green."

Amy: "I love those colors too. Maybe I can come over and see your room sometime and we can play your video game?

Follow up with these questions:

Do you think Sadie should let Amy come over to play her new video game?
How would you know if Amy's favorite color is pink?
Do you think Amy really likes Sadie or does she just want to get to know her so she can play the video game?

The important underlying question derived from the above example, that you can ask to open up a discussion is: "How can you tell if someone means what they say?"

This is just a sample but there are many real-life examples children will offer you on a regular basis once you open them up to the awareness that people's words don't always match their motives. What is critical to try to teach your child is that she can listen to someone's words but that she should also pay careful attention to the other person's facial expressions, gestures and body language. Trying to decipher the true meaning behind someone's words is more critical than ever. With the use of technology becoming the primary source for communicating, people are lacking the critical visual clues of conversation that we rely on to decipher meaning and intent.

A major problem with texting and emails is that conversation can be misinterpreted because words on a screen lack intonation, expression or gestures to go along with them. The words, "I'm so upset" can have many levels of meaning. It means one thing if the person is upset about not getting invited to a big party, another if she got a bad grade and another if her dog just died. Without the visual clues being available, it is hard to get a clear picture of just how upset this person is.

Acting Out Mixed Messages

You can train conscientious listening by playing the following "acting" game. Begin by telling your child you want her to guess if what you are saying is true. Tell her that before guessing she should not only listen to your words, but also watch your body language.

You can start by having your expressed feelings match your words. "I'm so happy we are going to the movies today," can be said with a smile and some sort of gesture to express your enthusiasm. Then try to switch it up so that your facial expression and gestures don't coincide with the emotion you are speaking about. This will draw upon your acting skills, which I promise you will get better as you practice.

For example: You can say, "I'm so happy because I love to clean up spilled juice on the floor."

Ask your child; "Do you think I really am happy just because I said I am?" While laughing you can say, "My child is so funny. She broke all of my favorite dishes while playing restaurant."

Once she gets the hang of it, you can have her make up the situations and you can guess her feelings. She will love being silly and love trying to trick you.

Playing with Nonsense Words

A fun game to play that encourages imagination, creativity and silliness is to make up nonsense words. This will demonstrate to your child that words can often have a variety of meanings to them and that a lot of how we feel is our interpretation of the word. Try making up nonsense words that involve feelings. Mad and angry can become the made up word of *mangry*. Sleepy and bored can become *slored*. You can make up names for anything including the characteristics of two animals. What do you call a kangaroo that quacks? A *quackeroo*.

You can find good examples of nonsense rhymes and words in many of Dr. Seuss' books. Shel Silverstein's books feature silly poems and drawings. *Where The Sidewalk Ends, A Light In The Attic and Falling Up* are just a few of his classic writings. Here is an example of one of his poems. I like it because it demonstrates to children the universal principle of cause and effect. One receives depending on what one gives. It's a great poem to pull out when your child is screaming that someone is acting mean or something isn't fair, and you can see that the present situation is the direct result of her previous behavior.

How Many, How Many?

How many slams in an old screen door?
Depends how loud you shut it.

How many slices in a bread?
Depends how thin you cut it.
How much good inside a day?
Depends how good you live 'em.
How much love inside a friend?
Depends how much you give em.
Shel Silverstein

A great thing about word games is that they are fun to play and you can take your words anywhere. I encourage you to turn off the music and DVD's during car rides and start playing with words and language. Your child, seeing you being playful, will be encouraged to play along. Children offer you the amazing opportunity to play and be silly and get away with it, all without judgment. As an adult, you have the best of both worlds. You can have all the playfulness of youth with the wisdom of maturity. Follow the games with a serious discussion. Ask your child if she can ever remember a time where she said something different than how she felt at the time? Did she ever feel scared and said she wasn't? Did she ever want to say *no* but felt pressured to say *yes*? This will bring the point of the game back into real life context for her.

The more you encourage discussions at any level, the more your child will come to you to talk. Building a foundation of mutual trust through your conversations will allow for open dialogue on any subject. This is one of the single most important parenting gifts you can offer your child. It should be your goal to build a feeling that she can trust what you say. It is essential to be authentic in your responses without allowing your own judgment to silence her. This will encourage her to build the habit of seeking you out for conversation and advice when troubled or confused. The gift these conversations will offer will be reciprocal. They will create a bond built on mutual respect and love that you will share over a lifetime. Children don't stop seeking advice just because they grow into adults. How many of you still seek your parent's advise or approval for your own decisions? Your child's trust in your supportive listening will offer her the comfort that she is never alone in her decision making process. By practicing conscientious listening, she will have the skills and intuition to make good decisions based on trained listening skills and instincts.

CHAPTER 8

Parenting Without Judgment

"The judgment of the intellect is only part of the truth."
CARL JUNG

Ruiz's second agreement to not take anything personally is key to seeing and accepting your child as a unique soul and a separate being from you. You will have a great deal of influence in sculpting who she becomes, but how she incorporates your input is up to her. This agreement forces you to leave your ego in the delivery room. Ruiz says, "Nothing others do is because of you. What others say and do is a projection of their own reality, their own dream. When you are immune to the opinions and actions of others, you won't be the victim of needless suffering."

Before you can begin parenting with this agreement in mind, it is imperative for you to consider in what ways you have allowed others' opinions, feelings, and feedback to effect you. Did you choose a career path that you felt would please your parents even though it wasn't your passion? Do you need praise in order to be motivated? Do you allow another's mood to influence your own? In what way would your own life have been different if you didn't take things personally? Would you be speaking to a long lost friend or relative whom you continue to hold a grudge against? Take a few minutes of self-examination to contemplate how you have allowed yourself to be influenced by taking things personally. Then consider how situations in your life might have played out differently if you didn't.

Most of us have been influenced throughout our lives by the fact that we *did* take things personally. Our feelings have been hurt, and our egos were wounded, leaving a residue of bitterness and anger that we carry around. When you take things personally, you give away a lot of your own power. You allow what others say and do to effect you. This agreement forces us to take responsibility for ourselves by believing in our choices and actions without the need to look to others for their opinions, approval or judgment.

Conversely, when we see others as separate from us, we don't allow their actions or words to hurt us. You will have the understanding that the guy who cuts you off and gives you the finger is not angry with you. You will see that his hostility has nothing to do with you and you won't allow it to effect your mood. This agreement offers you the opportunity to live your life grounded in your own belief system. It will also offer you protection from the hurt of allowing another's judgments, actions or feelings to effect you. This of course is easier said than done.

From a parenting perspective, this agreement will continually force you to live in a place of unconditional love for your child despite her behavior, accomplishments or limitations. Most parents want to hear praises about their children. Often the praise helps you through another long, difficult day. However, according to Ruiz, what others say or think shouldn't influence you in any way.

Do not allow your child's misdeeds or imperfections to define you. Inappropriate behavior doesn't mean you are a bad parent. Mothers often take their child's behavior and performance personally as a reflection of themselves and their capability as a parent. This is partly because throughout time, society has blamed mothers for their child's inadequacies. Today, many educated mothers who leave their professional careers are making their child's success their life's mission. This often results in feelings of failure if their child doesn't live up to the better-than-average expectations they have set for them. Judith Warner wrote in *Perfect Madness*, "Having over-invested emotionally in their child's achievement, she sees all this investment put in jeopardy when he fails at something." Do not allow the judgments of others, teachers, coaches or other parents, to define your relationship with your child. Labels are limiting. Even grades are subjective, and may be based on the teacher's personal perceptions, life experiences and mood at the time she grades the exams.

Do not blame yourself or others for making a bad-parenting decision. How could you know that the toy you bought was covered in lead paint, until after the fact when it was recalled? This agreement will force you to take responsibility for all of your decisions because you will not allow your decision making process to be influenced by others. When you make a poor choice, you will need to honor it as your best effort in the moment and not allow guilt to haunt you.

Do not allow your child's natural pace of development to define your parental abilities. Every child will move forward on her individual path at her own pace. You need to truly honor this. Just because your child's friend is reading at four doesn't mean you are not spending enough quality time with your child. Instead of blaming yourself, or looking for inadequacies that don't exist in your child, relish what your child is doing in the moment.

This is especially important if your child is born with special needs or limitations. Don't blame yourself. More than likely, nothing you did or didn't do could have prevented this from occurring. If you believe that everything occurs for a reason, even the most painful situations, then ask yourself what is the life lesson for me, and those around me that this child is offering? Is this situation bringing me into contact with other people I normally would never have met? Is it testing my worst fears and weaknesses, forcing me to grow beyond my perceived abilities? What is the positive from this negative situation for me, for my child, for her siblings and my marriage?

Often the life lesson to be learned from a child's illness or limitation isn't for the one who is afflicted. It's for those who have to care for and nurture the child. Stay strong and dig deep into your heart to examine your faith, your compassion and your ability to take and follow directions from someone more powerful like a medical professional. Acknowledge the ability to feel powerless over something out of your control. Once you accept the situation for all it has to offer, you see it as a blessing and not a curse. From this positive attitude will come strength, courage and the ability to cope with what you need to face adversity with dignity and grace.

CHAPTER 9

Children Need to Discover for Themselves

"Mistakes are the growing pains of wisdom."
WILLIAM JORDAN

As parents, it's instinct to protect our kids from danger. This works well as we are able to childproof our homes, feed them only the food we deem healthy and even choose the friends we bring into their lives. As they grow older and begin to navigate the world, we can no longer be by their sides. Yet, this need to want to protect them from hurt and painful experiences still exists.

What I have experienced is that children often interpret something based on the developmental level they are able to comprehend. For example: When I was pregnant with my second child, my son asked me who decided if a baby was a girl or boy? My first response to him was that God decided, but that wasn't specific enough for my inquisitive five-year-old. He then asked how does God decide? At that point I concluded that the concept of God was too vague and I responded with the facts. "The mommy has an egg and the daddy has a sperm. Together they make a baby. There are girl sperm and boy sperm and whoever gets to the egg first wins!" The concept of a race was something he understood. He was totally satisfied with that explanation and didn't ask for any further details.

As adults, we often bring our adult interpretation to a situation. In my class, I have observed two toddler boys kiss each other smack on the lips out of pure affection, while their mothers' faces turn red with embarrassment as their friends make snide remarks. The mothers perceive the situation from their preconceived notion that it still isn't culturally acceptable for boys to kiss one another. These children are just acting out of love. If they want to kiss a friend, then they do. They respond in the way that resonates with their feelings. They haven't been burdened with the labels and stigma that society has taught us to accept as adults. That is one of the treasures of childhood. The ability to be spontaneous, live in the moment and live from the heart.

Our assessment of a situation comes along with all of our own experiences as a filter. Our interpretation of events is often laden with our own emotions. If you experienced a teacher humiliating you in front of the class as a child, then you most likely will relive that pain and humiliation through your child when she comes home and reports she was scolded by her teacher for talking too much.

Our internal state at any given moment filters our perceptions. It determines and alters our external experiences. You are most likely more tolerant of your child throwing a tantrum if you have had a good night's rest than if you are exhausted from a sleepless night.

As difficult as it is, if we allow our kids to suffer through the small trials and tribulations of childhood, then when they are adults they will have the confidence to be able to handle what the world presents to them. If we are constantly trying to protect them from hurt, fix their problems before they begin, and intervene on their behalf in their relationships, then we are not really teaching them anything. They will only learn dependence on us and no matter how omnipotent we are we can't be every-where, for them, all of the time.

This following story about a butterfly, little boy and guru is attributed to the author Henry Miller. The message is strong and clear. Struggling is part of the natural growth process.

"Once there was a little boy in India who went up to a guru who was sitting and looking at something in his hand. The little boy went up and looked at it. He didn't quite understand what it was, so he asked the guru, "What is that?"

"It's a cocoon," answered the guru, "Inside the cocoon is a butterfly. Soon the cocoon is going to split, and the butterfly will come out."

"Could I have it?" asked the little boy.

"Yes," said the guru, "but you must promise me that when the cocoon splits and the butterfly starts to come out and is beating it's wings to get out of the cocoon, you won't help it. It is important not to help the butterfly by breaking the cocoon apart. It must do it on it's own."

The little boy promised, took the cocoon, and went home with it. He then sat and watched it. He saw it begin to vibrate and move and quiver, and finally the cocoon split in half. Inside was a beautiful damp butterfly, frantically beating its wings against the cocoon, trying to get out and not seeming to be able to do it. The little boy desperately wanted to help. Finally, he gave in, and pushed the two halves of the cocoon apart. The butterfly sprang out, but as soon as it got out, it fell to the ground and was dead. The little boy picked up the dead butterfly and in tears went back to the guru and showed it to him.

"Little boy," said the guru, "You pushed open the cocoon, didn't you?"

"Yes," said the little boy, "I did."

The guru spoke to him gravely, "You don't understand. You didn't understand what you were doing. When the butterfly comes out of the cocoon, the only way he can strengthen its wings is by beating them against the cocoon. It beats against the cocoon so its muscles will grow strong. When you helped it, you prevented it from developing the muscles it would need to survive."

So, the next time you do something for your child that she can do by herself, take a breath, pause and watch her struggle. It may take her twice as long to get herself dressed, but the joy she will experience in her accomplishment will be worth being five minutes late to school.

Remember: As painful as it might be to observe your daughter suffering because she didn't get invited to the popular girl's party, or your son didn't make the varsity football team, this is all a part of the essential learning process for him or her on the journey he or she needs to live through. It's not about you.

Motivational speaker and author Byron Katie, in her book, *Loving What Is*, has been teaching others how to examine their thoughts. She calls it "The Work. The work involves questioning your thoughts with four simple questions. Through her process she claims that you can find joy and peace by discovering the truth. She urges us to ask ourselves whose business we are in when we are in turmoil and stress. She writes that there are three types of "business" that any situation can be classified by:

1. **Your business**: These are situations that directly effect you and that you can control. (i.e. What you choose to eat and how you choose to feel).
2. **Other people's business:** These are situations that have nothing to do with you and that no matter how much you may want to change them, or the people involved in them,

you can't. (i.e. Your sister's husband is an alcoholic who gambles away their money).

3. **God's business:** These are situations that you absolutely have no control over like, natural disasters, sickness and death.

Katie claims that whenever you are in any type of business other than your own, you will loose 100% of the time and end up being frustrated, stressed and unhappy. Think how this philosophy might apply to your parenting style. As much as you may want to absorb your child's pain, you can't. If she is not invited to a party and her feelings are hurt, you can't demand that she be invited.

Before reacting to the hundreds of challenging situations your child will face as she moves along her journey, I encourage you to ask yourself, "Is this a situation that is your business?" Seeing yourself as separate from your child takes time and practice. It does for her as well. Try to see each situation that arises as a learning opportunity or as training steps for the bigger challenges that will follow. The best you can offer is to be supportive in your unconditional love.

CHAPTER 10

HONORING YOUR CHILD'S PERCEPTION - EVEN IF IT'S DIFFERENT FROM YOUR OWN

"What you see reflects your thinking. And your thinking but reflects your choice of what you want to see."

A COURSE IN MIRACLES

Perception is defined as the ability to see, hear, or become aware through the senses - it's the neurophysiological processes, including memory, by which an organism becomes aware and interprets stimuli. Its origins are from the Latin verb *percipere*, which means to 'seize or understand.' Often we think of perception as our way of observing the world. A broader definition includes how we physically interpret our environment using all of our senses. These perceptions are filtered by our emotions, beliefs and prior experiences.

Every perception of how we see and interact within the universe is a reflection of what first comes into our mind. Author Deepak Chopra wrote in *Power Freedom Grace*, "The world 'out there' may appear to be objective, but in fact the world is subjective; it is a construct of your own interpretations. You learn to interpret the world through your senses, and this brings about your perceptual experiences, including your experiences of the body-mind."

As adults, our perceptions are filtered through past experiences. A perfect example is if you have ever eaten anything and then gotten sick. The illness may not have been caused by the food, but just seeing or smelling that food provokes sensations of nausea and the fear that this particular food will make you sick if you eat it again. This belief is your unique perception derived from your personal experience. Since others have not had the exact experience you have had they also wouldn't have the association you do between that food and the sensation of nausea.

Parents have the power to influence our perceptions through the teaching of their preconceived ideas. These types of long-lasting beliefs that skew your perceptions can have an emotional foundation that may effect you for life. For example; every time you wanted to try out for a sport's team, your father told you not to waste your time. He said, "You won't make it because being a good athlete doesn't run in our family genes. You come from a lineage of thinkers not athletes." Because you weren't allowed to challenge your father's belief, you gave up thinking you had any athletic ability and never even tried to make a team. The results are that today, as an adult, you are overweight and have no confidence in your athletic skills. You can't contemplate or visualize yourself any other way than you are, so you don't even try to change. Your body has adapted to your vision of what it cannot do. Chopra also claims that "Your body is a field of ideas, and the body you're experiencing right now is an expression of all of the ideas you have about it." It is therefore a self-fulfilling prophecy that you are not athletic. You are living your current life from a pre-existing belief that your father planted in you many years ago.

Research by Dr. Bruce Lipton, author of *The Biology of Belief,* claims that by changing our limiting or negative perceptions, we can affect a positive physical outcome at the cellular level, promoting a healthier quality of life. Therefore, honoring your child's perceptions and beliefs, even if very different from your own, is critical in creating a physically healthy and emotionally well-balanced adult. Hopefully, this awareness empowers you to take control of limiting beliefs that you may have been taught about yourself and parenting; the world we live in and about your ability to effect change.

As always, this is easier to implement conceptually compared to executing on a daily basis in real-life situations. Here is a simple example: You see a red flower in your garden, but your child sees it as pink. No matter how hard you try to convince her the flower is red, her mind is telling her it is pink. It is her perception that is creating her awareness and experience. This discrepancy between how the two of you see a flower may be easy for you to accept. But, how do you react, as a parent, when the two of you experience a conflict with extremely different interpretations?

In this instance, you and your child are out shopping at the mall to buy new school clothes. Your daughter picks out a pair of designer jeans for $100. You pick out a store brand pair for $39.99. Your daughter contends that the designer jeans fit her perfectly. She insists that the $39.99 pair make her look fat. You argue that she looks just as good in the cheaper ones because there is no way you can justify, or afford, the designer jeans. However, she becomes increasingly frustrated and angry. You, too, are frustrated because in your mind the designer jeans look exactly the same on her as the cheaper version.

However, acknowledging that we all see things differently based on how we choose to see them, you can accept that she sees herself as fat in the cheaper jeans. You will have the understanding that she chooses to see herself that way, in order to justify buying the more expensive designer jeans she wants.

You can continue to argue your point in a hundred different ways, but you will not be able to change her perception.

Utilizing the awareness that you cannot change her point of view and that trying to do so is a losing battle, it is better to acknowledge her perception and feelings. Then, with sensitivity for her feelings of impending disappointment, you can make a different argument that she cannot deny. "Yes, you may think you look better in the designer jeans but as much as I wish I could, I can't afford the $100 to buy them for you."

Although she won't get the jeans she wanted, you validated her perception and desire while being honest about the reality of the situation. Even though she is disappointed in the moment, she ultimately will have more respect for you and the honesty of your relationship.

The egotistical notion that we all experience the world in the same way is one that many believe. It's not necessarily true that if I see blue then you see blue. If I experience danger, then you must too. However, this idea initiates conflict when we are not open to another viewpoint. Parents often take it personally, as a betrayal, when their child experiences situations differently than they do, resulting in anger and resentment.

The awareness that we perceive differently opens our minds to alternative ways of seeing and thinking. Here are a few games and activities that you can do with your children that will demonstrate how we all see through our perceptions.

Tunnel Vision

What you will need:

- **Piece of paper**
- **Pen or pencil**

Poke a small hole through the paper with just the tip of a pen. Have your child look around wherever you are and describe to you what she sees. Write down what she describes to you. If it is a familiar place like your home, make sure she understands that she tells you only the things she actually sees through the tiny hole, not the things she remembers being present in the space.

Next make a new hole slightly larger by poking the pen through the paper a bit further. Now have her look through the hole and describe what she can see. Have her compare what she saw through the tiny whole and through the big hole. You can have a conversation discussing how having an open mind is like looking through the larger hole. When your mind is really open, your eyes can open up to see and experience a lot more.

I Spy

What you will need:

- **Toilet paper tube to make a "spy glass."**

This game will promote observation and language. It will develop visual discrimination, the ability to focus on details and how to categorize objects. Deepak Chopra wrote, "Your sense of sight also profoundly influences your body. Research has shown that information you take in through your eyes can influence heart rate, blood pressure, stress hormones and so on."

Have your child look around the room and have her "spy" different objects. You can ask her to find all the blue things she sees if she knows colors. You can do this with shapes or any category of objects. This game will also help her to look carefully at details. You might ask her to close her eyes and then add a few small items to the space that were not previously there to see if she can find the new items.

You can take this game outdoors and go on a treasure hunt. Prior to going outside, make a list with your child of things you want to find. This will give you some insight as to what intrigues your child. Using her "spy glass," have her look for the "treasure" on your list. If she finds something on your list, you can bring it home and put it into a treasure box.

There are several series of books that train observation skills available for preschoolers through adult levels. The *I Spy* series by Jean Marzello and Walter Wick offers a child's board book edition and progresses to a difficult adult version. When my son was young, he loved the *Where's Waldo* book series by Martin Handford. For teens and adults, Al Seckel has created several optical illusion books such as *Ambiguous Optical Illusions* and *The Ultimate Book Of Optical Illusions.*

Rose Tinted Glasses

What you will need:

- **Toilet paper tubes**
- **Tape**
- **Scissors**
- **Colored cellophane. (You can purchase this at a craft store. This is available in the spring since it is often used to wrap Easter baskets. If possible, purchase several colors such as red, blue and yellow).**

Cut a small square of the cellophane large enough to cover the end of the tube. Cover one end of the tube with the cellophane and secure it with either tape or a tight rubber band.

Make a tube for each color of cellophane applying the same process as above. At the same time, cut out a small square of each color of cellophane and set it aside. Have your child look through the tubes to see the world in different colors. This is also a great way to teach colors to a young child. Place a tube up to her eyes and name the color as she looks through it.

Next, cover the red tube with a square of the yellow cellophane (that you set to the side) and ask your child what color she sees now. This is a great lesson in color mixing. With the yellow, red and blue cellophane, you will also be able to make orange, green and purple! The surprise and magic in this discovery will delight your young child since she might not have discovered the principles about color mixing.

A concrete way to teach your child we see things differently, is for both of you to look at the same object through a different color tube. Have your child look at an object through one color and you look at the same object using a different color. Have her describe what she sees. Now describe what you see. You can say, "Oh no that couch isn't red, it's blue." She may argue back that it is red because she is looking through the red tube. Swap tubes with her and it will become quite clear that the couch can now be blue!

For older children you can make this game more abstract by adding the dimension of feelings into the picture. Ask your child to use her imagination to associate a color with a specific feeling. What color does she see when she feels happy, sad or angry? For example, "When I am happy the world looks yellow with a beautiful glow." Or, "When I am sad the world looks grey with no light shining through it." For young children there is the book titled *My Many Colored Days* by Dr. Seuss that exemplifies the idea of connecting color to a feeling. For older children who understand this abstract concept of attaching emotions to color, they can create their own book.

You will have a lot of cellophane left, since it comes in roles and you will only need a small piece to make the above game. With some of your extra, you can make stained glass windows to see the outdoors through colors.

Stained Glass Windows

What you will need:

- Scissors
- Colored cellophane
- Clear contact paper

Cut out a square of clear contact paper. Cut out several small pieces of the colored cellophane. You can cut out different kinds of shapes such as triangles, squares or circles to make your windows interesting. This will also offer a shape lesson, too! Peel back the contact paper so that the sticky side is facing up. Have your child place the colored shapes of cellophane onto the clear contact paper. It is fine if she overlaps the shapes since this will create new colors and an interesting design. Once she is finished, seal the design with an additional piece of clear contact paper. Hang the stained glass window in one of your windows to perceive the world in colors! Your child can even make these as gifts.

Mood Windows

What you will need:

- Scissors
- Colored cellophane
- Clear contact

Cut out a piece of contact that will fit inside your window-panes. Cut out a variety of shapes from the same color of cellophane. Place the same color shapes of cellophane onto the contact. Do this for each of the colors of cellophane you have. Let your child label the colors with feelings such as, "The purple window is my silly window." "The green window is my quiet window." You can put these up in different windowpanes in your child's room for her to look through. If you don't want them in your windows, punch holes into one side and place them in a three-ring binder where she can pull them out to use when she wants to express her mood. You can call it, *My Color Mood Book.*

My Colorful Feelings Book

What you will need:

- **Several sheets of white paper or construction paper in an assortment of colors**
- **Markers, paint or crayons**
- **Stapler or string and a hole punch**

If you are using white paper, then begin by labeling the top of each sheet with a different color. If you are using colored construction paper, just place an assortment of colors on top of one another. Let your child pick the colors she wants to include in her book. Create your book by either stapling down the left side or punching three equally spaced holes along the left side. If using the holes, slip the string through each hole and tie a knot.

Have your child attach an emotion or feeling to each color. You can do this by using the appropriate color marker or crayon or selecting the corresponding color paper. She can write out words and draw pictures of things that represent her feelings of each color to fill the page.

In this way, you are teaching your child that the same things can be seen differently depending on one's "mind's eye." The idea that how we feel can effect what we see is a difficult concept. Attaching an abstract thing like a feeling to a color will begin to teach her that we see things differently depending on how we feel at the moment.

Through exploring these projects, children will learn that we each experience the world we live in very differently. This will open them up to understanding that we need to acknowledge and respect individual differences in others. This will foster acceptance. Reinforce that it's okay to love someone and think or feel differently than them. Then model this idea by honoring and accepting the ways your children are different from you without criticism

Experiencing Perception Through the Different Senses

Variations on perception can also be compared using other senses. Most parents of teenagers have experienced a difference in perception regarding how loud music is played. You can get a sense of how your child hears things by playing the following game.

Music: Loud and Soft

Create a playlist to include a variety of music such as rock and roll, country, jazz and classical. You can also just use your voice. However, your child might prefer music since she has to listen to you all of the time!

What you will need:

- **A variety of music**
- **Paper or cardboard**
- **Markers**

Write the words "Too Loud" and "Too Soft" onto separate pieces of paper. If your child can't read, draw a recognizable symbol to represent too loud and too soft or like and dislike. Try a thumbs up or down symbol or a happy or sad face.

Begin playing the music. Slowly turn up the volume and tell your child to hold up the sign when it gets too loud. Do the same thing for too soft. This will give you an idea of how she hears things.

Then you take a turn. Let her be in charge of the volume and you show her the signs. This will give her an idea of how you hear things. Talk about how you hear things the same or differently.

Next play different types of music. Have her hold up a happy or a sad face depending on if she likes the song or not. You can also have her dance if she likes it a lot or sit down if she dislikes it a lot. Then once again switch. Let her be in charge of which song she chooses to play.

You can also play these games in a group with several children at a time. This will display how they can be friends but like different things. This will also demonstrate to your child that the differences between what people like or dislike aren't connected to being a grown up or a child.

Taste Testing

You can also explore differences in experience with the sense of taste. Remember the story of *The Three Bears*, when

Goldilocks thought the dad's porridge was too hot, the mother's too cold and baby bear's was just right? Explain to your child that everyone likes different foods. At the grocery store, let her pick out a few new things she never tried to eat before. Select a few for yourself, as well. This is a great way to urge her to try something you have been trying to introduce. Encourage her to pick from different food groups such as some nuts and beans or cheese and fruit.

When you get home, prepare the new foods that need cooking or washing and line them up. Each of you can taste the new food and hold up the happy or sad face. Let her go first so she is not influenced by you. You can also explore differences in tastes by adding seasonings, herbs, or honey to foods she already eats. Try applesauce, mashed potatoes or plain yogurt. Add spices like cinnamon, or even basil, to the same food to change its taste. Follow the activity with a conversation reinforcing that it is okay to like different things than other people, even if those people are in your own family. No one is right or wrong. We are all unique and we have to respect each other's differences.

Smelly Fun

You may be familiar with the term "aromatherapy." It is the use of plant oils, also called essential oils, for psychological and physical well being. It is most often associated with spa treatments or candle scents. The science behind aromatherapy is that varying smells produce a physical response in the body. Two of the most common aromatherapy scents on the market are lavender to help you relax and promote sleep and eucalyptus to help open blocked nasal passages.

You can create your own special aromatherapy blends. Before you take on this endeavor it is important to be aware that many oils are too potent to be used around children. Essential oils should also never be used without a carrier such as water or witch hazel. A great resource that will educate you on aromatherapy and what oils are safe for specific age children is *Aromatherapy for the Healthy Child* by Valerie Ann Worwood.

You can purchase essential oils at organic food stores and they may be able to guide you in deciding what to buy. The oils and supplies such as small bottles are also available through several websites

Essential oils are potent. Most recipes will only need a couple of drops of each oil. I recommend you share the cost with a friend to purchase several oils to make a variety of recipes. Below are a couple of child-friendly recipes:

Sweet Dream Spray

Ingredients:

- **Equal parts of lavender and chamomile essential oils and witch hazel**
- **1 oz. of distilled water**
- **1 small, clean spray bottle**
- **Mix the ingredients into the bottle.**

This is a nice spray to use if your child is having a difficult time falling asleep. You can spray it into the air or directly onto her pillow. It will create a sweet, relaxing aroma. If she is having bad dreams or expressing a fear of going to sleep, you can tell her that this is a magic spray that gets rid of bad dreams.

Beddy-Bye Bath Oil

Ingredients:

- 1 oz. almond or jojoba oil
- 2-3 drops of lavender
- 1-2 drops of chamomile

Mix together and shake well. You can also mix a few drops of this blend into a cup of milk and add that to the bath. This will create a relaxing tub time in preparation for a good night's sleep.

Bath Tea Bags

What you will need:

- Heat seal tea bags available on websites that sell essential oils.
- Lavender buds or
- Rose buds or
- Peppermint leaves or
- Chamomile flowers

This is a fun activity that you and your child can make together. Choose what type of bath tea bags you want to make and purchase the necessary botanicals. Have your child place a small amount of botanical into the tea bag leaving enough room for you to close the top with a hot iron. Keep the tea bags in a sealed plastic bag to maintain their freshness. You can then create decorative labels for the different types with cute names on them. Lullaby Lavender, Peppy Peppermint or Rockin Rose are a few suggestions. These make wonderful gifts.

CHAPTER 11

ACCEPTING YOUR CHILD AS A UNIQUE INDIVIDUAL SEPARATE FROM YOU

*"In order to be irreplaceable,
one must always be different."*

COCO CHANEL

All sensory activities have the goal of offering you and your child the opportunity to explore how differently we each experience the world. Allowing your child to experience things differently from you, on a concrete level, will offer her permission to open her mind to abstract ideas and new ways of experiencing life without the fear of reprimand. It also is training for you, too. Many parents are threatened when their teenagers come home with a different vision for their lives than the parents have regarding their personal goals, religion, and choice of friends. If you create an atmosphere of acceptance for your child, respecting her uniqueness and differences, she will be more likely to include you in her exploration process. Later on, in her teenage years, you will not be caught saying, "I had no clue," or "I never knew." Instead, I hope you will smile and say, "We are really different but I love her just the way she is."

Honoring our children's uniqueness, separate from our own, is an essential first step in allowing them to find their true selves. This awareness is critical not only in meeting their physical needs, but emotional ones as well. It is also an important parenting skill in recognizing the differences between each of our children. You only need to parent more than one child to know that each and every child is unique, presenting quite different challenges than the prior one. Successful tactics that worked for the first child will more than likely fail for the second. This is part of what makes the parenting role so challenging, but also so rewarding.

Acknowledging that our children are unique individuals often means leaving our own ego and expectations at the door. Statements by your husband to your child like, "How can you not like basketball when I love basketball?" Or you questioning, "How can you hate chocolate when I would give anything for a Godiva?" have certainly left many a child perplexed and exasperated.

This is a story that exemplifies the idea that our children experience the world separate and different from us. Recently, I had the opportunity to elaborate this point to my neighbor Diane. We live side-by-side on an extremely busy street with nonstop traffic. We've had many discussions about my frustration fighting with the town about the noise the manhole covers make when the cars roll over them.

For the past year and a half, she and her now two-year-old son Jack, have been part of my mommy and me program. Since I have known her, she has complained about Jack waking at 4:30 am every day, leaving her exhausted and depressed. Because my first son didn't sleep through the night until he was five, I can totally empathize with her frustration. We talked about a few tactics, but nothing worked.

Recently, I got the idea to purchase a white noise machine to drown out the *clump, clump* noise made by the manhole covers that was keeping me up every night. Surprisingly, it worked! It was the best purchase I made and I am pleased to say I am no longer fighting with the town and I sleep like a baby.

About a week later I woke in the middle of the night with the pressing thought I needed to tell Diane about the sound machine for Jack. The next time I saw her in class I said, "I had a thought late last night that the sound machine might also help Jack. I think it's pertinent that he wakes at 4:30, the same time the cars and trucks begin to travel the morning commute, making a racket as they roll over the manhole covers." "Really," she said, "I never hear them. Molly, my oldest daughter, sleeps in the same room as Jack and doesn't have any sleep issues." Diane's subtle inference was that if it didn't bother Molly, how could it bother Jack? I responded by saying, "My husband sleeps in the same bed as I and doesn't hear the noise, but I do."

I could see her ah-ha moment. Maybe it was possible for her son to hear the traffic while she and her daughter didn't. I explained that perhaps his hearing was more sensitive or maybe he was a lighter sleeper. For whatever reason, she should consider that Jack could possibly experience the same situation quite differently than the rest of the family. With this realization came the sparkle of hope that maybe the machine might actually work. She left saying she was definitely going to buy one.

As individual beings we can only experience the world from our own perspective. As we mature, this perspective is tainted by our experiences and beliefs. Why, then, as parents, do we think we always know what our child feels or experiences? In certain situations it is important to get out from behind our ego and try to experience the situation from a different perspective, from our child's point of view. If our child says she is full after two bites of dinner and we respond with, "No you can't be. You have to finish your food," then not only are we contradicting her judgment, we are disrespecting her feelings.

Inadvertently, we are teaching her to tune out her physical sensations. If a child says she is full and doesn't want to eat, then you should honor that. Maybe she is not feeling well. Maybe she is too excited with her new toy to think about eating. The fact is that by acknowledging her statement as true, we are honoring her feelings, showing her we trust her to know her physical sensations and make her own decisions. Starting off with the small decisions like whether to finish a meal or not will allow her to trust her instincts when needing to make the larger choices in life. It will also help you to respect her choices all along the way.

As parents, we want to make so many of the decisions for our children so they won't fail or experience pain. When they get older, we expect that the ability to choose and decide correctly will magically appear. Making appropriate choices is a learned skill based on knowing oneself and testing the cause and effect principle of those choices. If you allow your child to begin early with the simple decisions, the big ones won't be so overwhelming later on.

Abstract Art

What you will need:

- **Construction paper**
- **Paint**
- **Painting Utensils (optional)**

This activity is designed to demonstrate how you and your child can interpret something differently. Allowing your child to experience a situation from her own perspective will encourage her to be her true self.

Lay out a large piece of paper and explain to your child that you are going to create a painting together. Tell her not to try to paint anything specific. Instead, each of you will blend the paint colors using your hands or painting utensils by taking turns. Mutually decide when the painting is finished. Once it is dry each of you will have a turn to interpret what the picture is and explain why you believe it is so. You can enhance this activity by rotating the painting to see if this creates a different interpretation.

You can elaborate on this idea by Googling "Abstract Art". This will offer you the opportunity to introduce your child to many famous abstract artists and their paintings.

Finish My Story

What you will need:

- **Imagination**
- **Pen and paper (optional)**

This activity will foster imagination and build your child's confidence in expressing her own ideas. It will create an opportunity for each of you to honor the other's ideas building mutual respect.

Begin by describing any type of open-ended situation. You can do this verbally or by writing it down. Once the scene is established, ask your child to finish her story. If you are writing your stories, you can finish them at the same time. If you are telling the stories verbally allow your child to go first to create an ending. Then you take your turn. Discuss why she chose her ending and offer why you chose yours.

Here is an example of a *story starter*:

It was a sunny day in May and Meghan and Lily were walking home from school. Suddenly, an unleashed dog ran across the street and started following the two girls.

When thinking of a *story starter* create a brief scenario that includes open ended elements. For example, you don't know what relationship the girls have to one another. You don't know if the dog is lost or if his owner is close by. You don't know if the weather is going to change or remain the same.

If you have difficulty in coming up with an idea you can always refer to pictures in magazines to inspire you. Any story will foster conversation, quality time together and the opportunity to respect each other's unique ideas.

CHAPTER 12

HONORING YOUR CHILD'S TALENTS AND INTERESTS

"Not knowing when the dawn will come, I open every door."
EMILY DICKINSON

Every child is born with the birthright to endless potential and infinite possibilities. Children will discover their innate passion through exposure, participation and positive experiences. As parents, it is normal to introduce them to the activities we love and interest us first. If you were raised by the water and spent a lot of time sailing, you are likely to get your child on a boat long before someone who never experienced the love of sailing.

As a parent, you have your own personal visions and dreams for your child that may turn out to be very different than the one your child has for herself. It takes a self-assured parent to allow a child to follow her own passions without being threatened. Never discourage your child's dream as foolish or impossible. It is often the adults in a child's life who restrict dreams and limit potential. The adult's fear of the child's failure can cause a parent to place limits on a child before she tries. Children may set enormous goals for themselves such as, " I want to be in the Olympics." The child may be exceptional at her sport, but the parent may try to tame her aspirations by saying, "Getting on an Olympic team is very rare. It's almost impossible because it only happens every four years." Unfortunately, trying to protect your child from something that hasn't occurred yet is placing limitations on her potential before she even gets started trying to accomplish her goal.

If a child is always supported then she will be encouraged to try new things without the fear of failure, ridicule or persecution. True success is to wake up everyday and love what you do. Remember, life is a journey and we are all on our own path at our own pace. Most of us won't take the direct road to where we want to go. It may be more like a maze with several dead ends. However, the side streets offer us the experiences we need and the lessons to be learned that will eventually lead us to the place determined by our heart's desire.

There are many factors that will ultimately effect your child's success. Some are in our control, but most are not. In Malcolm Gladwell's book *Outliers,* he discusses the process of birthday cut-off dates as life changing effects on children in sports and academia. He sites research by Canadian psychologist Roger Barnsley who discovered that the very best Canadian hockey players, from the first squad of the A travel team to the National Hockey League, had birthdays in January, February or March. This, he says, is because the eligibility cut-off date to play in Canada is to be ten years old by January first. This gives the child born in January the opportunity for more practice over a child born in November who is not eligible to play until the following year. The January child also has a size advantage over the boy who is ten months his junior and less physically mature. Gladwell wrote, "If you make a decision about who is good and not good at an early age; if you separate the 'talented' from the 'untalented;' and if you provide the 'talented' with a superior experience, then you're going to end up giving a huge advantage to that small group of people born closest to the cut off date."

This same bias of older children succeeding over their younger counterparts is also true in education. This is a critical piece of information for many parents who struggle with the decision of whether to keep a child back from kindergarten if her birthday is in the later part of the year. In many states, the cut-off date is the first of September which means that many parents of children born in the summer months which are close to the cut off date, struggle with the choice to enroll their child in school or hold the child back.

As it turns out, research has overwhelmingly proven that it is wise to hold them back since the disadvantage younger children face doesn't go away. Gladwell wrote, "The small initial advantage that the child born in the early part of the year has over the child born at the end of the year persists. It locks children into patterns of achievement and underachievement, encouragement and discouragement, that stretch on for years and years."

Proof of this shows up overwhelmingly in a variety of test scores. Older children in the same grade and of equal intelligence consistently score better than their younger classmates. This can have life-changing consequences from being accepted into a variety of programs, to being placed into a specific track or level of course work that can ultimately determine college options.

Another contributing factor effecting a child's experience and success is who they are exposed to. My husband is a sports nut. Therefore, he naturally wanted all of his three children to play sports. Not only did they have to play, but he also became their coach. This involved choosing players for the league's teams. After attending his first coach's meeting, he came home disgusted. He reported that choosing the town basketball league's teams had resembled more of a political sports machine than an organization designed to offer fun for children through playing of the game.

The men in charge were made aware, in advance, of the playing potential of each child from his or her prior league experience. Children were identified by their skill rather than their name. They were traded and fought over by these grown men who had reduced their vision of these eight-year-olds by the quality of their play and potential wins for their team. They never considered that an unknown child might possess more talent than one of their researched players.

Because of the coaches pre-assessment and pre-judgment, the reputation of the known talented children earned them the opportunity to further excel over their less-skilled peers. The good players got more playing time by the coaches, which earned these players more practice. This allowed them to become better players. They excelled over their "not so good" teammates each successive year. After the first year, the not-so-good players didn't stand a chance of becoming one. This kind of type casting can have life-long emotional consequences and can even create a change in the outcome of a child's life. I had this experience with my son Jake.

When I was a single mom, I tried my best to offer my sons many adventures and opportunities. However, I was told by my dad that my boys needed to be involved in a team sport to experience what it felt like to be part of a team surrounded by other boys. So I registered my son, Jake, for a Saturday morning basketball league when he was in first grade,

The first Saturday he trotted off quite excited. He loved his new shirt that hung down below his knees. When I picked him up after practice and asked him how it was, he said, "Okay". The following Saturday he complained about being too tired to go. I insisted he had to go because he was part of a team and they needed him to play, thinking I was teaching him the importance of teamwork. Off he went with much prodding. The third week they were playing a game, so I went to watch and cheer him on. Mostly, I observed him sitting on the bench for three-quarters of the playing time. He obviously wasn't one of the players the coaches fought over. It was excruciatingly boring for me, so I can imagine what it was like for an energetic six-year-old to idly sit while his teammates were out there having fun playing. After the game, I asked him if he had fun. He reluctantly said, "It's okay." The following week, he hid under the coffee table refusing to come out when it was time for practice.

After much arguing, tears, yelling and self-induced stress on my part, I gave in. I didn't make him go, but I felt guilty about it. I was tormented by his pleading with me to not go and my preconceived belief taught to me by my own mother that "If you start something you need to finish it." I struggled with this pre-existing belief, remembering all of the times my mother forced me to go to lessons I didn't want to attend because she signed me up for them. This process of forcing me to go only ended up with me being resentful in the long run.

There are so many small decisions you will make as a parent that you will second-guess later on. You might even try to go against your parental instinct because you think it is the right thing to do. This was the conflict that tormented me. But then I asked myself, why? Would I want to be made to do something I disliked so much that it forced me to hide under a table? Saturday was one of his two days off from school. Why shouldn't he be able to spend it doing what he liked doing? I didn't make him go back. The abhorrent thing is that the coach never even called to see where he was!

Whatever activity your children are drawn to, it is essential to support them without your own desire or unfulfilled needs getting in the way. Unconditional acceptance and unconditional love is what we are all seeking from our parents. How may times as a child, or even as an adult, have you done something that you didn't really want to do just to please your parents?

Know that most children will sacrifice their own dreams if they know you disapprove. However, it will ultimately create stress and conflict. Unconditional love for our children begins at birth. Over time, we allow the pressures of our competitive society to place demands on that love by creating expectations for our children. When our children fail to meet those expectations, whether realistic or not, we often give them mixed messages about our approval and acceptance. Every so often, ask yourself honestly, "Do I love and accept my child unconditionally?"

How do you discover your child's passion and talent unless you expose them to a variety of activities? Exposure is the tactic that most parents take. I have seen children signed up for gymnastics, music, swimming, art and a foreign language all before they are two! This method is not only expensive, but is overwhelming for the child and exhausting for you.

I suggest that one of your roles as a parent is to expose your child to activities through initially exploring them together. Instead of rushing to sign up for little league, first throw the ball with your child. Does she like it? Is she enthusiastic? Does she ask to do it repeatedly or does she have to be prodded? It is only through doing that one learns and discovers what they are good at and what they like. As Aristotle wrote, "Pleasure in the job puts perfection in the work."

Use your observation skills to watch what she enjoys. Is she always asking to draw? Is she always upside down? Does she love building things with Legos? Observation is a valuable commodity that will offer you insight into what intrigues her. However, it takes time. You cannot begin to observe your child's natural interests if she is always being rushed between structured classes with no down-time to explore what she truly likes.

Often children will offer you many clues to how they are experiencing the world. Careful observation and connecting the clues may prevent you from many wasted hours and dollars on activities that just don't fit with your individual child. At two, Matchbox cars fascinated my eldest son Ben. He would spend as much time as I would allow lining them up, moving them back and forth and observing their wheels. He would have me repeatedly read books on all types of cars until the pages were falling out and I thought I would go crazy from the repetition.

As he got older, he began to build large Lego sets. He was able to differentiate the differences in size and shapes of even the tiniest of pieces and follow the sequential steps it took to build a $100 Lego kit that took hours to complete. In elementary school, he moved on to building large models, the type that required glue and lots of patience! At 11, he built his own computer with a friend.

From the time he was a toddler, he was giving me clues as to the way he saw, and interacted in, this world. He was never interested in any of my many attempts at arts and craft projects, and was less interested in competitive sports. Although I always supported his endeavors, I cannot say I knew where he was headed. It wasn't until he insisted on applying to only one engineering college that I finally connected the dots and had an *ah-ha* moment. It now made perfect sense to me. From childhood, his passion is what guided and motivated him to become who he is today, a mechanical engineer, loving what he does.

Utilizing this awareness and respect for individual differences, allows your child the opportunity to do her best with your encouragement. The word encouragement broken down into its root meaning is *en* from the French "to put in," *courage*, also from its French roots, means "heart or innermost feelings." So to encourage is to *put in with heart*.

Praise, on the other hand, is given after the fact. Praise actually comes from our own ego because it requires our judgment. Before one offers praise for an accomplishment, one needs to see it as worthy of praise. What you deem worthy may be quite different than another, based on your own expectations.

To offer your child your heartfelt support without expectations for the outcome is to truly encourage her. This will allow her to take risks that will challenge her potential because she won't be afraid of failure. New situations or difficult tasks can be introduced as opportunities to learn from, rather than experiences to excel in.

This may be hard for you to do since we all want our children to avoid the pain of failure. Often we tend to intervene when we see that a situation is becoming too frustrating or difficult for our children to achieve with success. Instead, focus on what they have already accomplished and offer reinforcement for past successes.

For example, your son strikes out on the last play of the baseball game and his team loses. He is obviously upset, and his team members are angry, giving him dirty looks as he walks off the field. In that moment, your heart is breaking for him, but instead of saying it is only a game and he will have another chance next week, acknowledge his disappointment by reminding him of his accomplishments. "I know you're really upset because you struck out, but I also know you gave it your best effort, just like you did earlier when you caught the fly ball and prevented a run from scoring. You were great then, and I know your teammates appreciated your catch." This type of encouragement will offer your child support while giving him permission to fail.

Here is a fun activity that will help your child identify the things she likes to do. You and others in the family can define your interests at the same time. This will be a concrete, visual way of seeing what things you like as individuals and what things you like as a family.

What We Like Poster

What you will need:

- **Paper**
- **Something round to trace a circle such as a CD or a large bowl.**
- **Pens, pencil or markers**

Do you remember learning about sets and intersecting sets in math? We will use the same format. Begin by placing the large side of your bowl onto the page and tracing the outer rim. You will need as many circles as you have family members. However, you will need to create an overlap or intersection of each circle with another.

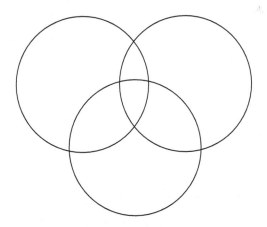

Above is what a family of three would look like. Have your child write down the things she likes within her circle. You and your partner do the same. Look and see what activities are identical. Include those in the intersection between Mom and child if you share matching interests, and Dad and child, if they share corresponding interests. If only you and your partner like an activity, write it in the intersection between the two of you. If you all share the same interest, then write the activity in the intersection of all three circles.

Try not to intervene until your child is finished with her list. What she chooses to include might surprise you. This will also pinpoint activities you might want to do together as a family, especially if you have more than one child and each child's interests are very different.

This is a little variation on the above theme. It's an activity that will demonstrate how each of us has something special within us. Sometimes this is hidden to others, but it is there for each of us to discover in our own way, in our own time. It could be a talent or interest like those mentioned above or, something intangible like our imagination, our energy or our enthusiasm. Whatever it is, it's what makes each of us unique.

Hidden Gem

What you will need:

- Balloon
- Small stone
- Acrylic paint
- Glitter
- Empty plastic water bottle

Have your child pick out a small stone and allow her to paint it any way she wants. Make sure the stone she picked will be able to fit through the top of the bottle. You might try to find gold or silver paint if you don't have glitter. While it is drying, cut the bottom off of the water bottle to create a plastic funnel. Once the paint is dry, stretch the mouth of the balloon over the end of the water bottle. Drop the stone into the bottle and it should slide into the balloon. Once the stone is hidden inside the balloon, blow it up and tie a knot in the end of the balloon.

Explain to your child that the balloon represents her. You can even let her decorate the outside to look like herself, if she chooses, with some markers. Discuss how everyone has something special about him or her, but others can't often see it. Sometimes, we don't even recognize it about ourselves for a very long time. You can end the activity with a conversation about how what is inside us makes us unique and is essential to define us, not our physical appearance.

Exploring Geodes

Another exciting way to demonstrate that we all have hidden qualities or talents not seen from the outside is to make an example of a geode. From the outside, geodes look like ugly round rocks. But if you crack them open, they can reveal beautiful crystals inside. Geodes are formed from fluids, which crystallize in cavities within a rounded rock. You can buy small kits for under $10 at a craft store. This will provide a fun family activity. Kits will contain more than one geode so if you have more than one child, each child can have his or her own to open. Opening involves placing the geode within a sock or towel to offer protection as you hit it with a hammer. They usually crack open easily.

Once again discuss how you can never know what is inside someone from the outside. See if you and your child can come up with examples of people you know that are different on the inside than what they appear on the outside. I have a friend who at age 72 has white hair, wrinkles and an elderly man's jowls; however, he acts younger than many of my 50-year-old contemporaries. He works every day as a carpenter, which requires a great deal of strength. He dresses like a man half his age in spandex black tee shirts and designer jeans when he goes out to dinner. He is married to an attractive, slender redhead who is 30 years his junior and is a perfect example of someone whose physically aging exterior doesn't match his youthful energy level or mindset.

CHAPTER 13

Never Assume You Know

"All our knowledge has its origins in our perceptions."
LEONARDO DE VINCI

Assumption is defined as something that is accepted as true or certain to happen, but without proof. It is the "without proof" that is critical to remember as a parent. When you are ready to blame or accuse one child over another, or judge a situation or others, remember to get your facts first. Being informed with correct information, prior to reacting, should be the main criteria for you to maintain throughout your personal life and your parenting years.

Ruiz suggests that one way to avoid making assumptions is by asking questions to acquire accurate information. Clear communication is essential to this process. This will enable you to attain the facts to assess a situation and respond appropriately with the correct knowledge.

I would encourage you to leave the first common parenting assumption at the maternity ward. It's the one that says that professionals always know what is best for you and your child. Although professionals can be a blessing, there is a lot to be said for parental instinct. I can't begin to tell you how many times over the thirty years I have had as a parenting educator that a mother instinctually knew something was wrong with her child while the professionals proclaimed she was overreacting or insecure. Often the mother's intuition was confirmed after many visits to the doctor and numerous tests. No one will hold your child's interest to heart as close as you. Do not assume that just because a professional has a prestigious degree, he or she has better judgment or all the answers.

Don't assume your child understands what you are saying or feeling. Children are quite literal and may take your words for their concrete meaning rather than their implied message. Once, while teaching, I asked a group of toddlers to look out the window to see what kind of day it was. Taking my words literally, one of the toddlers got out of his chair, walked across the room, and climbed up onto another chair so he could peer out of the window. I couldn't scold him for leaving his seat since he responded literally to my request, just as he heard it. Be direct and specific in your communication. It's imperative to say what you mean and mean what you say. It will save you much aggravation in the long run.

Don't assume that just because you asked for something to be done it will be. Equally as true, just because you may ask your child not to participate in certain behaviors, do not assume that she will comply. In order for your child to respect your demands, she first has to respect you. This will come from the consistency between your word and your actions. Often as parents we take the easy way out. For example, while you are running around doing five things at once in preparation for your book club members to arrive, you ask your child to pick up her toys. She continues to play ignoring your requests. As the time approaches for your guest's arrival, and you have asked her ten times to pick her things up without a response, you give up on her cooperation and angrily pick up all the toys for her.

In that moment, cleaning up for her was the easiest and quickest way to accomplish your goal. However, this simple scene sets up a long-lasting dynamic between the two of you. She learns that if she continually practices her selective hearing, she can avoid doing what she doesn't want to do. It teaches her to disrespect your wishes and you. This interaction may appear harmless when it comes to cleaning up toys, but the dynamic will remain and could be potentially dangerous when you tell her not to go to a particular party because you know there will be drinking there and she goes anyway.

Don't assume you know everything about your children or their friends. You are not a mind reader and they can be very good actors. For decades, children have quite cleverly covered their tracks. I am sure most of you have some hidden secret about some mischief you did that even to this day you haven't exposed.

When I was about four years old, I heard my baby brother awake in his crib. Since I was awake and bored, I decided to go into his room to play with him. I lowered the side of his crib and tried to lift him out. Unfortunately, I dropped him and he fell to the floor screaming. I immediately ran back to my room and pretended to sleep through the entire ordeal. He lost a tooth from the fall. Luckily for me he was too young to tell. I didn't reveal that secret until I was well into my adult years.

Some of you might remember the classic 1960's television family drama show "Leave It To Beaver." The character Eddie Haskell was best known for his contrived flattering remarks towards Mr. and Mrs. Cleaver every time he walked into the house and said "Hello, Mr. Cleaver; hello, Mrs. Cleaver." He was obviously trying to impress them with his stellar manners in the hope of winning their approval. Your child will make many friends and acquaintances over the years. Some you will be able to read like a book, while others will easily have you fooled as to their authentic character, like Eddie Haskell. Instead of making assumptions about your child's friends based on their academic standings, their parent's occupation, or which neigh-borhood they live in, spend time to get to know the friends your child brings home.

Your child's peers will be extremely influential in her choic-es, actions and beliefs. It is often one of the things that parents fear. There's always the potential of your child falling into the "wrong crowd" and having her life ruined. You will never be able to choose your child's friends for her. Hopefully, the values you have tried to instill from birth will guide her to choose peers who influence her in a positive light. However, once she introduces them to you, try to establish a relationship based on mutual re-spect through conversation that is non-judgmental and accept-ing. Her friends will feel a sense of trust and acceptance from you and be more likely to reveal their authentic selves. This will allow you to remain connected by learning about the friends she chooses through consistent and continuous interaction.

Don't assume you know what your child is doing, thinking, and feeling or that you know where your child is. No parent is a mind reader. Only open communication will offer you in-sight into how your child experiences a situation or honestly feels about something. When children are small they are easy to read. We don't have to assume anything because they give away all the clues. They haven't yet learned to hide their emo-tions or cover their tracks.

As children grow they become socialized. They learn the principle of cause and effect and that there are repercussions for their behavior. Instinctively, in self-defense, children will learn to be a master of disguise if they feel threatened. It's the fear of authority and punishment that encourages them to lie and live in disconnection to their true selves. They may often claim to be in-nocent of a deed when they are truly guilty: For example, if they are pretending to be daring when they are truly scared or claim-ing they did their homework when they haven't opened the book.

By continually showing them unconditional love, your children will learn your love is not based on their behavior. Remind them that certain actions are unacceptable, but that you are always supportive and present for them. Children will repeatedly test your patience. When they do something wrong, remind them that you dislike their behavior but still love them. Establishing an honest relationship from the start with your child based on open conversation will eliminate the need for you to make assumptions about her life and behavior. Your goal is to always remain a part of her journey, accepting the information she has to offer without judgment. By doing this, you will facilitate this process.

Assumptions can create false expectations if they are based on inaccurate information. This can often leave you feeling foolish when you realize you created your own idea of something that wasn't reality. This happened to me regarding a student referral to my school. I taught a lovely family whose two boys attended my program over several years. Their skin was white and they each had blonde hair and blue eyes. I'll call them the Carters. Their mother phoned to inform me her husband's cousin, also a Carter, had just adopted Asian twin girls and the mother, Eva, would be calling to enroll them. I thanked her for the referral.

Eva enrolled the twins by phone and when she arrived on the first day I was surprised to see she was Asian. My initial assumption was that Eva was a white woman who had adopted Asian twins. This wrong assumption was rooted in the belief that because the Carter family was white-skinned the cousin married a white-skinned woman. I was wrong. I thought to myself how great it was she had the opportunity to adopt children who resembled her.

The children were absolutely adorable and a bundle of energy which required Eva to bring another adult. A few weeks later, she said that her husband wanted to attend. This is a big event in our mommy and me program since it often takes a bit of courage for a dad to come into a class with 11 women.

The following week, the twins' father arrived and to my surprise, he was Asian. I stood there perplexed since I knew that the rest of the Carter family was white. I realized what a fool I was in making my original assumption that he was white skinned just because his cousin was white skinned. Of course, the answer to the riddle is that the Carter family, who is white, adopted the twin's dad, who is Asian, when he was a child. The sweet side to this tale is that the dad was adopted from the same orphanage from which he adopted his twin girls. Hopefully, I was able to hide the look of surprise and contain my embarrassment and humiliation, which in my mind created false expectations based on wrong assumptions.

Assumption is the root of all prejudice and judgment. We see a person of a different nationality and, right away, we make assumptions about his intentions and character based solely on our inference. Most often these assumptions are based in fear and years of social conditioning. Our behavior has to model the one we want to teach. If we want to teach our children acceptance, then we need to accept others for who they are. Making judgments in front of your child about another's lifestyle based on his clothes, skin color, or career choice models bigotry and hatred.

Several years ago, a black man was walking down the center of a prestigious Boston suburb when he was stopped by the police for questioning. Few black people lived in this community. As it turned out, much to the embarrassment of the police, he was a Boston Celtic basketball star out enjoying the afternoon with his wife. Regardless of whether he was a sports celebrity or not, the person who called the police made the assumption that this man was up to no good based on his skin color. Her wrong assumption created humiliation for the individual, the town and its residents.

Modeling acceptance of others by minimizing our assumptions will help our children to eliminate prejudice and hatred towards others. All children are born with love in their hearts for everyone. Prejudice, judgment and hatred of others, based on assumptions, are learned behaviors that we often teach unknowingly through example. Be cognizant of what you say about others in front of your child and impeccable in your word when giving answers to their questions about why others are different. Children always seek your honesty. If you give it, you will be pleased to receive it back from them.

Making Assumptions from Photographs

What you will need:

- **Photos of people in a variety of situations expressing various emotions**

Show your child a photograph and ask her to tell you a story about it. If your child can write, have her write down her thoughts about the picture. You do the same. Then compare both of your interpretations. For example: The photo is of a child crying in the park. Your child's interpretation may be that the child in the photo fell down and hurt herself. Your interpretation may be that the child didn't want to go home when her mother said it was time to leave. Discuss how one can't assume which interpretation is right because they both could be right.

You can make this more of a game by finding photos where the situation is explained. These could be from the Internet or a newspaper. Separate the photo from its caption. Have your child write down or tell you her interpretation of the photo. Then confirm if she is correct or not. See how many interpretations she correctly interprets. Follow the game with a discussion about how there are many things we see and interpret without having all of the facts. This is why we can't make assumptions because without the facts, our assumptions can lead to misunderstandings. Encourage her to find out the truth and facts about a situation through good communication before developing her opinion or belief.

CHAPTER 14

KARMA AND DISCIPLINE

"What you are is what you have been.
What you'll be is what you do now."
BUDDHA

The law of attraction is based in the fundamental principle of karma. The word karma originates from the Sanskrit word *karman* which means deed, action, effect or fate. Karma is not our destiny or fate since we always have free will. Instead, karma is the direct result of previous actions or thoughts. It is the purest form of cause and effect. In his book *The Twelve Principles of Karma*, Steven Hairfield defines karma as "a genuine, natural, unrelenting Law of the Universe, the mechanism through which gives us experience as the Law of return action."

The concept of karma originated from ancient Eastern philosophy and later became a key component in the religions of Hinduism and Buddhism. According to Buddhist theory, every time a person acts there is an intention behind that action that originates in the base of the mind. It is the intention, rather than the outward appearance of the action that determines the karmic effect out in the universe. For example, someone who donates large sums of money anonymously would reap positive karma from his actions compared with another who donates with the intention of creating a memorial for himself. This type of giving is self-serving and would not reap the same positive karma since it is the ego that motivates the giving rather than genuine generosity. Although karma has its roots in eastern religions, the belief that we reap what we sow is cited in the Bible in the book of Genesis in the Old Testament and in the Galatians 6:7-9 in the King James Version.

Madame Chiang Kai-shek, first lady of the Republic of China explained karma this way: "If the past has taught us anything it is that every cause brings its effect, every action has a consequence. We Chinese have a saying: If a man plants melons, he will reap melons; if he sows beans, he will reap beans. This is true of everyone's life; good begets good, and evil leads to evil. True enough, the sun shines on the saint and the sinner alike, and too often it seems that the wicked prosper. But we can say with certainty that with the individual as with the nation, the flourishing of the wicked is an illusion, for, unceasingly, life keeps books on us all. In the end, we are all the sum total of our actions. Character cannot be counterfeited, nor can it put on and cast off as if it were a garment to meet the whim of the moment. Like the markings on wood, which are ingrained in the very heart of the tree, character requires time and nurturing for growth and development. Thus also, day by day, we write our own destiny; for inexorably...we become what we do."

Today, the concept of karma shows up in many New Age philosophies and has even made its way into the mainstream vocabulary of the twenty-first century. I recently heard it in a marketing campaign around holiday time. An ad encouraged children to give holiday gifts to underprivileged children in order to create "good karma." The mainstream definition of karma is that "What goes around comes around." Simply put, if you cut someone off in traffic today, then you can be sure that someone will cut you off in the future.

Although the concept of karma is supported by the idea of reincarnation, it's not necessary to believe in reincarnation to benefit from the lessons of karma. What karma teaches us is that every human is responsible for all of the events that occur in his or her lifetime. Everything, both good and bad, joyous and painful, happen to teach us a lesson in the exact way our soul needs in order to evolve.

For most of us, particularly children who are too often heard saying, "It isn't fair," this idea is empowering. Because if we believe in karma, then we can never see ourselves as victims. Everything that happens to us occurs from a place we created from our thoughts, our actions and our past behavior. The past can be yesterday, last year or a prior life. The point is that the occurrences that happen today are a result of our prior behavior. What better belief can you have as a foundation for teaching children self discipline?

Karmic debt is the term that implies that the residue from all of your negative deeds and thoughts will carry over into another lifetime to be corrected. Karmic debt can be accumulated in many ways. Most often karmic debt is acquired by doing someone harm through our relationships in a prior lifetime. But it is also accumulated through our behavior and actions. Karmic debt is not a punishment, although it may often feel like it since it requires us to live through uncomfortable or painful life experiences that we must correct.

The purpose of karmic debt is to provide a lesson for a soul to learn and evolve. For example, if a man cheats on his wife in this lifetime, destroying his marriage through his deceit, then in his next lifetime he will experience the pain of someone deceiving him. The lesson doesn't need to be offered in the same scenario. It may not be an affair, but it could be that a business partner cheats him out of his profits, ruining his business and leaving him to suffer in poverty. The karmic debt he acquired through cheating on his wife in this life will require him to experience someone deceiving him in the future. Even though it is a different scenario, he is still learning the pain of deceit and losing something important to him.

In one of my Tarot card readings, I was told that in a prior life I had a relationship that caused another to financially lose everything. Therefore, in this lifetime it was my karmic debt to experience material loss, including all of my money, as I had caused another to do in a prior life. The lesson for me was not to grow too attached to material things and learn how to start over again. This has been true in my life. More than once, I have had to start over financially from scratch!

You can teach the idea of karma and karmic debt to your children without having to get into the idea of reincarnation if this is not in line with your religion or acceptable ideas. The basic premise is that there is a cause and effect to all of our actions. My mother used to say, "God sees everything and if you do something bad, then he will punish you." Sure enough, after I misbehaved, if I hurt myself or had something bad happen, she would remind me that God was punishing me because of what I previously did wrong. Unfortunately, this placed the fear of God in me as being the all-knowing disciplinarian ready to retaliate when I misbehaved. Karmic debt is the idea that you can't escape your own bad behavior. Instead of an all-knowing threatening God, karmic debt insinuates that the universe is aware of your actions and will respond accordingly by providing life lessons to improve yourself and evolve.

There is another belief about karma that says the same lesson will continue to be played out throughout your life until you learn it. That is why some individuals often find themselves repeatedly in the same negative situation. They are not learning their life lesson. This is an incredibly powerful belief. One might say it is one of the principal laws of the universe. The belief in karmic debt can encourage us to be conscientious of the effects of our choices and behavior. Hopefully, this awareness will motivate us all to be our best.

To learn more about karma, I highly recommend you read Steven Hairfield's book the *Twelve Sacred Principles of Karma*.

Utilizing the Principles of Karma as Discipline

Why teach the principle of karma to children? One great reason is that it will help them understand that their behavior has direct consequences. It is the philosophy behind the principle of cause and effect. If I do this, then I can expect that to follow. Your child may not feel the consequences right away, but she will begin to understand that what she does, her intention and how she does it will create an effect on her life. This awareness empowers your children with choice. They can choose to behave badly, but they will also have to experience the consequences of those choices somewhere down the road.

From a practical sense, one of our responsibilities as a parent is to teach our children how to behave properly according to acceptable norms in society. Usually this is accomplished through discipline. Reward the behavior you want to see continue, while you punish the behavior you want to stop. This system is based on classical conditioning. Often, with children, this type of suppressive punishment/reward system feels unjust, leaving a child feeling powerless and resentful towards the authoritarian, which most often is you.

However, with guidance, we can allow our children to discover the ramifications of their actions on their own. For example, growing up, my mother had a rule: "You had to go to school unless you had a fever or were throwing up." Well, there are a great many varieties of illness where one may feel awful without fulfilling these two requirements. As a result, there were many days when I was forced to attend school, congested, or with a stomachache, or just exhausted.

Needless to say, I highly doubt I really learned anything of substance on any one of those days that I was forced to attend school, other than to resent my mother for forcing me to go while feeling lousy. Besides resenting her, our ability to trust each other was diminished. The underlying message she conveyed to me was that she didn't trust my judgment about my physical symptoms or my word about how I felt. I, on the other hand, believed that she didn't care about me, trust me or have my wellbeing at heart.

When my own children grew old enough to express their discomfort about not wanting to go to school, I decided on a different tactic that would give them control over their symptoms and offered the opportunity to be empowered. I told them only they knew how they felt since it was their body. However, if they wanted to skip school that day, then they had to make up the work they missed. They also understood that sick children don't magically get better in the afternoon at the end of the school day when their friends get home. So if they skipped school, it meant they couldn't play with their friends on that day. The result was that rarely did my children choose to miss school unless they were really ill. They decided it was too hard to make up all the missed work. Missing school was also honored if they just needed a "personal day off" like we adults need every now and then from our stressful routines.

If a child understands that her behavior always has an effect on her self and others, then ideally she will be able to monitor herself rather than being policed by an adult. According to karmic principles, this is called the law of integrity; how one behaves when no one is watching. If we want to teach children how to make good choices, we have to allow them the opportunity to experience choosing. This is true even if it means letting them make some bad choices with negative ramifications along the way. This is an essential part of the learning process. A three-year-old who is just beginning preschool will quickly learn that hitting other children is a sure way of not having any friends to play with. An eight-year-old who cheats on a test will learn the humiliation of getting caught and having to take the test over again using only her own knowledge. A teenager will learn what it feels like to be sick to her stomach after she drinks too many beers at her first big high school party.

Through independent exploration, a child will determine for herself how negative behavior creates its natural response as punishment. This interactive process will offer her ways to understand through personal experience what behaviors are acceptable. Her conclusions will come from within. This will result in her appropriate behavior being self-sustaining, since her actions are the result of her own consciousness and not dependent on your reprimand.

Practicing Making Choices

You can set up situations in a playful way that will encourage your child to make conscious decisions that will teach appropriate behavior. Or, you can wait for the universe to naturally present one of these situations to you, which shouldn't take very long. As children develop their sense of self, they will want to demonstrate their autonomy. This will result in them challenging you. The important idea I would stress for you to keep in mind is to convey to your child that you love her unconditionally, but her behavior has to be appropriate. Education of the heart is your biggest responsibility as a parent. When your child believes in your unconditional love, she will then feel secure to be and live as her true self in the world.

Choices that Teach Sharing

For preschoolers

If you have two children, set up a situation where you have three of something. A perfect example is three cookies for the two children. It could also be one of something they both need like a marker for an art project. Ask the children, "Look, I have three cookies and there are two of you. What should I do with the third cookie?" Wait and let them respond. If they are equal developmental age you should receive a similar type of response. An older child will have the developmental capacity to better understand the situation at hand and may be able to come up with several solutions to the same dilemma. Obviously, the answer you are looking for is to split the third cookie in half to share. However, if you don't hear that response, be grateful because you are being given a "teachable moment" to explain why that is the right, thoughtful and fair thing to do.

For grade schoolers

As your children develop, they will quickly learn the art of negotiation. My son, Ben, learned this so well that he mastered how to wear me down to get what he wanted with his reasoning abilities. I was aware that he was doing it and yet I still caved most of the time. Giving in left me feeling guilty and left him with way too much power. Believe it or not, children will challenge you but they want and need you to be in control to feel safe.

Here is an example of a way to use the principle of karma when your child is insisting they need or deserve a new outfit, computer game or bike. You are rushing to the checkout line where you ran in to purchase new vacuum cleaner bags. You have fifteen minutes before you need to pick up your oldest at gymnastics. As you pass by the audio isle, Sam, age eight declares, "Look, Mom, they have the new computer game I want." You are so rushed you barely respond, but then Sam stops dead in his tracks and won't move.

Mom: "Come on. We have to go right now."

Sam: "But this is the exact game I want and if we don't get it now they will sell out. It just came out yesterday."

Mom: "Sam, there is no way I can afford to buy you that video game."

Sam: "I don't care. I need it. All my friends will have it and I won't be able to play with them online if I don't get it."

Mom: "Sam, if I buy that game for you now, we won't have any money to go to the movies this weekend. I promised your sister and dad we would all go as a family."

Sam: "I don't care about some stupid movie."

Mom: (*Introducing the idea of karma*) "That sounds very selfish. How do you think that will make your sister and dad feel if we don't have any money to go because I spent it on something just for you? Being selfish will create a lot of negative karma for you. If you act selfishly now, then sometime in the future someone will be selfish towards you and how do you think that will feel?"

Sam: *Struggles with the idea and reluctantly puts down the game.* "I guess I don't want to have to deal with something disappointing in the future because of wanting some computer game now. I'll wait."

Mom: "I'm so proud of your good choice. It's hard to let things go when you want them. But, I know that by doing the right thing now, something good is going to happen for you in the future. We don't know when, but it will."

Both Mom and Sam walk out holding hands without the computer game. The result is that Sam feels empowered by his choice and doesn't resent his mother for not purchasing the game since he came to his own conclusion about choosing not to be selfish. Mom feels good because she didn't give in but also doesn't see herself as the "bad guy."

In situations that involve siblings who are able to wage verbal warfare, the key is to take yourself out of the negotiation process. Offer your children the opportunity to work difficult or frustrating situations out on their own. This is not a simple task. They will use every tactic to try to engage you into their conflict. This is a lose-lose situation for everyone, because as soon as you open your mouth, you will be seen as taking sides. Every child wants her parent's undivided attention and love. They will seek out your loyalty to their cause with Herculean strength. Don't fall for it.

Instead, remind them about the principles of karma. If they use mean words now, someone will use similar words against them later and they will not only experience how bad it feels but also they will have caused it to happen. If they don't share now, then in the future they will experience the frustration of wanting something they can't have. Point out that there will be a reaction from the universe to all of their negative words, thoughts and actions. Even if they don't say something mean, make sure they know that if they are thinking they hate their sister, then that negative thought will still have impact on their future.

You can intervene, by simply asking, "Is that good karma or bad karma you are creating?"

Yo-Yo Karma

What you will need:

A yo-yo

One of the simplest ways to visually show karma is through the use of an old fashion yo-yo. Explain to your child that the yo-yo can demonstrate to her how karma works. Explain that the yo-yo can represent her thoughts or her actions. Show her that whatever she focuses on, says or does, will come back to her just like the yo-yo does when she pulls on it. You can even make up a game of stating an action (*the cause*) as she lets it spin down and the effect of the action as it is pulled up. Begin with stating an action as the yo-yo goes down and having her respond whether it is negative or positive karma as the yo-yo comes up. For example, when someone takes something that doesn't belong to her it creates negative karma. When I share one-half of my lunch with a friend who forgot hers, it creates positive karma.

After you are sure she understands the difference between positive and negative actions, you can make it more challenging. State the action on the way down and the resulting karma on the way up. For example, as she lets the yo-yo spin down say," I share all of my toys with my friends." As the yo-yo comes up you can say, "I have lots of friends who like to play and share with me." As the yo-yo goes down, from a negative perspective she can say "I lied about doing my homework." On the way up she can say, "I am going to get in trouble at school" or "It will be hard for you to trust me about my homework in the future."

A variation on the game would be to have the person with the yo-yo state the cause or action, and the other person shout out the effect or karmic result before the yo-yo gets back up.

You can also demonstrate karma with a party favor blower. This will be easier for younger children. What goes out comes back at you. You can purchase these at a party store. This is a fun, inexpensive way for several children to learn about karma at the same time.

Principle of Mirrors

One of the principles of karma is that what you do is reflected back to you. It's called the principle of mirrors. Here is a fun craft activity to demonstrate this concept:

Reflective art

What you will need:

- Paper
- Several colors of paint
- Paint brush or other utensil (spatula, spoon, sponge, fingers)
- Small mirror

Explain to your child that whatever she does or thinks will come back to her in some way. Explain that it may not happen immediately but the universe will know. Ask her if she can give you an example of what you are trying to convey. If not, then provide one for her. A positive example is, "If I share something of mine with others, then something good will happen to me in the future. From a negative perspective, "If I gossip about one of my friends to another one of my friends, then she won't be able to trust that I can keep her secrets in the future."

Here is another activity to teach an older child that everything in the universe is reflected back at you. To do this, you will need to purchase a small mirror. Teaching stores often have small rectangular mirrors used in classrooms that are non-breakable. You might also purchase a purse-size mirror. Explain to your child that all our thoughts and actions are reflected back to us by the universe. If we think negative, angry thoughts, we will attract angry people and negative situations into our lives. However, if we fill our minds with peaceful, loving thoughts, we will attract positive experiences into our lives.

Fold a piece of construction paper in half and ask your child to paint only one half of an object on the paper. She can paint half of an apple or half of a house. Let the painting dry. Then hold up the painting to the mirror and see it reflected as a full drawing. It's a fun example of how what we do is always reflected back at you.

You can also place a small object in front of the mirror like a piece of jewelry or utensil. Ask your child to show you the object that is real. Then reinforce that all of her life is a reflection of how she thinks and acts just like the object's reflection that looks exactly the same as the real thing.

If you don't have a small mirror, you can create reflective art by giving your child a piece of paper. Fold it in half to create a crease and ask your child to paint only on one side of the page. Fold over the unpainted side onto the painted side. Gently press down and re-open the paper. You should have a copy of the original painting on the other side of the paper. This represents the mirror principle – that what you do is recreated back to you.

The following activities will take more time and effort to make and experience.

Kite Strings and Karma

Most children love kites. Most adults do, too. There is something light and freeing about the sight of a colorful kite dancing in the sky. You can enjoy the experience of flying a kite together with your child while teaching her a lesson about karma. The experience of flying a kite is one that you usually remember throughout your life, so you will be creating a wonderful memory with this activity.

What you will need:

- **A kite with a small hole punched into its tail**
- **String or yarn**
- **Several plastic cups**
- **Scissors**
- **Marker**
- **Small stones**

Make a small hole into the bottom of each plastic cup ahead of time. Cut a very long piece of string, enough to string together all of the cups you want to use. Pull the string through the bottom of the first cup and make a large secure knot so it will hold the cup in place. Then attach the cups by running the string through the bottom of each one. Don't forget to make a large secure knot under each cup to allow the cups to be upright with a separation between them. Leave at least 4 inches between each cup. The knot needs to be on the inside, under the cup, otherwise they will all just fall on top of one another. You will need to tie the knot prior to running the string through the bottom of the next cup. The goal is that you are trying to create a long tail of cups, which should be heavy enough to pull the kite down, especially if they have stones inside of them!

Next, show your child the cups. Ask her to suggest things that might create negative karma. Some examples are being selfish, hurting someone else's feelings, stealing or lying. Write one of these negative actions onto each plastic cup. You can then ask her to fill each cup with one or more stones. You can even ask her to determine how many stones the action is worthy of depending on how "bad" she sees the action. For example, lying may be represented by one stone but stealing equals three stones. This will be a good opportunity for you to see in a concrete way how she views the morality of specific actions. You can then pack the cups inside one another for travel until you are ready to use them.

Begin by saying that the kite is going to represent her and the cups are going to represent bad karma. Explain that when we act positively we feel great, light and beautiful. We have the potential to go as high as we want and accomplish the things we dream about because we are free from negative karma.

Next, you need to get the kite into the sky. Sometimes this is easier said than done. After flying it for a while, explain that when we do negative or bad things we create negative karma that attaches itself to us and weights us down. Pull the kite down low enough so you can attach the cups to its tail. Now try to let it up and see what happens. It should be more difficult to get the kite up as high as it was without the cups because of the "negative karma" attached to it.

Last, you can suggest there are ways to correct negative karma through apologizing, forgiving yourself, acting properly and being kind to others. Snip each cup off, one at a time, and watch the kite start to soar, once again, without the weight of its negative karma dragging it down.

Karma and Weights

If flying a kite is not an option for you, then you can also use the same principle that negative karma "weighs you down" by using some sort of weight tied to your child's foot. Explain that bad karma is something you drag around that limits you from being happy and the best you can be.

What you will need:

- **Ankle or wrist weights or several large washers strung together or full-unopened cans**
- **Masking tape**
- **String**
- **Scissors**
- **Paper or self-adhesive labels**
- **Markers**

Explain to your child that when we do negative things that hurt other people or make them feel bad, we create negative karma. Remind her that like attracts like. Give her an example of the ramifications of a bad behavior. For a young child, start off with an example she will readily comprehend. "If you don't share a toy with a friend, then most likely that same friend won't want to share a toy with you." For an older child, you can put a little distance between the action (cause) and its effect (karma). "If I cut in front of someone in a line, then more than likely someone will do that to me one day, too." You can ask her to give you an example to make sure she understands that her actions have ramifications for others, the universe and ultimately back to herself.

Now write out some negative actions onto the labels. Use issues you may have been dealing with in your child's life. This will be a non-threatening way to address these issues. Lying, cheating, not sharing, being selfish or disrespectful are just a few most parents have to face at some point.

Place the labels onto the cans. Tie one end of the string to your child's ankle. Then wrap the string around the can and secure it with the tape. Have your child try to walk while dragging the attached can. You can continue to add a can by wrapping the string around each one and taping it so it stays in place. You can have your child do a variety of things with the cans or weights attached to her like trying to climb up the steps, run outside, or put on her pants. Have her do anything you can conceive of to make the point that when we do hurtful or bad things, the resulting negative karma stays with us, weighs us down and makes life more difficult.

If you feel you do not want to use cans since they are apt to scratch floors or get dented, you can also use a paper chain to symbolize carrying the karma around with you. To make the paper chain you can cut thin strips of paper approximately 2 x 6 inches long. Write the actions onto one side of each strip. Make your first loop and attach it to itself with tape. Then slip the second strip through the first and tape it closed. Continue this to the desired length you want to create. Your child won't feel the "weight" in the same way but it might be more realistic for you to enact.

Karma Cause and Effect

What you will need:

- Cardstock paper
- Scissors
- Markers

You can make this into a fishing game by adhering self-adhesive magnets to the back of the karma strips and using a strong magnet to try to attract the karma.

Cut out from the cardstock 2 inch x 2 inch squares. On each of the squares, write out an action. This should include positive and negative behaviors. Next, cut out 1 inch x 4 inch strips of cardstock. On these strips of cardstock, write out the words *positive karma* or *negative karma*. You can also coordinate the positive and negative to a color, red means positive and blue means negative. This will help children who can't read.

Place the action cards into a pile. Allow each child to take a turn either fishing out an action or pulling one from the pile. Then take turns matching the card to its corresponding karma. You can also change the game by dealing out the positive and negative karma strips to each child and have each one find actions that match what they have been dealt. So if I randomly get three positive and one negative karma strips, I would have to try to pull three positive actions and one negative action to match them. Here are some examples of actions you may want to include on 2x2 inch cards:

Positive karma: I donated all of my old toys to the local shelter. *Negative karma*: I didn't tell the truth about breaking the window.

Negative karma: I thought mean things about my sister.
Positive karma: I offered to help Mom carry in the groceries without being asked.

This is a great opportunity to teach desired behavior you are trying to encourage in your family in a subtle way. If you are trying to get a specific point across to your children, make sure you write those behaviors or thoughts onto the cards. For example, if you are trying to encourage your children to clear the table without being asked, use one of the cards to write: "I help clear the table without being asked." This creates positive karma. If you are trying to stop teasing between siblings, you can write, "I like teasing my sister." This creates negative karma.

If your children are able, allow them to create their own behavior cards. This will offer them an opportunity to play out negative behaviors they might think of doing but don't such as: "I cheated on my history test," or "I ate all of the cookies."

One last suggestion is to make sure you not only include behaviors on the cards, but also thoughts. This will reinforce that negative thoughts can also create negative karma. For example, "I wish my brother would run away and never come home."

Through these fun activities your children will recognize that their thoughts and actions create an effect out in the universe in a concrete way. They will also learn that the repercussions for their thoughts and behavior, both bad and good, are experienced for quite sometime. This is especially true for our bad choices where the results may not be felt for years in the future.

Offering your children this knowledge empowers them in their decision-making ability, and in how they choose to behave since they will comprehend that everything they do has a direct effect on how they live their own lives. It also allows you some freedom from always having to play the role of policewoman or referee.

CHAPTER 15

ALWAYS DO YOUR BEST

*"Let yourself be silently drawn by
the stronger pull of what you really love."*

RUMI

The idea of always having to do your best may feel overwhelming. But before you begin to contemplate this agreement, understand that doing your best means giving it 100% with the resources you have at the time. The demands of parenting, for all that it entails, with household responsibilities and job obligations, are going to drain you of physical and emotional energy. Accept this as truth and give yourself permission to be not perfect.

What you do with the energy resources you have on any given day is what is essential. The same question asked twenty times might not irritate you one day but drive you crazy the next. There is no judgment of how much energy you should have or what is in your reserves. Everyone is different. Marianne Williamson wrote in her book, *A Return to Love*, "There is a feeling of inner peace that comes from total relinquishment of judgment. We don't feel the need to change others, and we don't feel the need to be different than we are." It is always the intention behind your actions that is most important.

Abigail's mom may be able to coach soccer, be the Brownie troop leader, and work part time, whereas you may be overwhelmed by the responsibility of deciding what to make for dinner each night. Accepting your own limitations is the first step to living in synchrony with your natural rhythm and helping you manage your days without stress. If you truly can handle getting your children to only one activity on any given day, then admit it and never schedule the second, because I guarantee that after the first activity, no one will be able to enjoy the second if you are stressed from getting there. German author Johann Von Goethe wrote, "The man with insight enough to admit his limitations comes nearest to perfection."

Just as you need to accept your own limitations, it is also important to acknowledge your child's individual style of living in this world. Some children can move quickly from activity to activity while others become overwhelmed when asked to do too many things in a short time frame. Some children absorb new information as if by osmosis; others need to labor over new ideas before they incorporate them into their understanding. The awareness of respecting your child's unique strengths and weaknesses will allow you to honor her place in the world without comparing her to other children. You don't want to be compared to Abigail's mom, nor does your child want to be held up to the accomplishments of your best friend's child down the street.

Whether it be cooking dinner, presenting at a meeting or reading bedtime stories, do it with the best intention that you are able to summon at the moment. That way, when you look back on your life, you can truly say that you did everything with your best effort.

By living with the awareness of always doing your best, you will offer your child a realistic role model of how one can live life taking on challenges without being tied to the outcome. She will see that sometimes Mom has a lot of energy and is very patient and sometimes she is very tired and yells a lot. She will learn to honor your humanness by witnessing your moods and mistakes.

Ultimately, not being the perfect parent will give your child permission to fail and not have to be "perfect" to please you. Without the pressure of being perfect or having to live up to high expectations, she will be more willing to take risks and challenges. When she makes a mistake and is upset, remind her how much you still love her just like when you make mistakes she still loves you. This will help her understand that love isn't dependent on an outcome. It is a permanent source within each of us that we can count on being there.

In our competitive society it is quite difficult to allow oneself the freedom to evaluate your performance based on effort. From a very young age, children seek positive reinforcement from their parents and adults in their world. As a parent, I encourage you to encourage your child with a full heart for all she dreams to do, and praise her always for her effort.

There is a distinct difference between the concepts of praise and encouragement. Praise occurs after the act has been completed. It originates in our ego because it has a judgment assigned to it. We only offer the praise if we think the action was worthy of it. Encouragement, on the other hand, occurs prior to the start of the action. Its purpose is to inspire and motivate from love and is not dependent on the outcome or result.

Back in the 1980s, parents were told to use positive reinforcement to build his or her child's self esteem. It was the new approach proclaiming that through positive reinforcement, parents could motivate children to stretch their abilities, take risks and become successful. Decades before, the consequence of a child's behavior was attributed to the child. Scolding was presented as "bad boy" or "bad girl." The new approach required the adult to offer praise or dissatisfaction for the action of the child rather than assigning the feedback to the child. This was supposed to enhance the development of the child's self esteem.

As a new parent, I was more than willing to offer praise for every little action my son attempted. I remember saying things like "good walking," "good eating," and "good listening." Parents of the 1980s used these non-stop compliments to encourage their children to perform even the most basic skills. The problem in rewarding activities that don't require much effort is that it doesn't encourage a child to stretch her limits. If a child is looking for external rewards as a motivator for her actions, then what happens when there is no one there to watch?

A perfect example of this is when a toddler runs across the room only to fall flat on her nose and often, before she has barely even hit the floor, her mother runs over to pick her up asking, "Are you all right?" with panic in her voice. This usually results in the child screaming at the top of her lungs, with crocodile tears until Mommy makes the fall "all better" with a kiss and hug. (There actually is no real "boo-boo.") However, if the same child falls in the same manner and no one responds, she will usually take a peek around, pull herself up and continue on her way. Most children will look for your reaction before they decide on their reaction.

This type of falling down occurs in my classroom about 20 times a day. It has gotten to the point that sometimes I respond with a loud "touchdown" when the child falls which usually evokes a startled look at me and then the child gets right on up and continues playing. One day, I did this and after shouting "touchdown," the little boy jumped up quickly with his arms straight up parallel to his ears, the symbol the referees use to declare a valid touchdown in a football game. His dad had one up on me and made his falling down into a game. Needless to say it was adorable and evoked a lot of attention for the getting up and not for the falling down. After all, this is what is important to teach children even at a young age. It's not about the falling down because we all do it, but it is the way in which one gets up that will determine one's success!

In retrospect, the results of praising every little action our children attempted or accomplished, was that we created a generation of self assured, oversized egos who often expressed a sense of entitlement. What is entitlement? According to author Maya Angelou, "It is a consciousness of *I deserve*. It is feeling we have the right to rewards, special privileges, or recognition based on personal merit, achievement, or simply because of who we are. It's having a sense of superiority, as in, 'I have so much experience, you should listen to me.' " These children had no problem with possessing positive self-esteem. In fact, they thought they were good at everything and became easily frustrated when a task required too much effort.

They often blamed their failures on external reasons like, "The teacher was so stupid and couldn't explain anything." "It was the other guys' fault that I smashed into the curb because he stopped short." Parents raising children from the perspective that their child was amazing, were often willing to support the child's theory of external blame, taking on the school, Little League coach or whomever else got in the way of their child's success. Unfortunately, the parent didn't look within him or herself to see that the child's way of interacting within the world, and others, was at least in part created from their parenting style.

There really is no blame since the parents of the 1980s, including myself, were following what we believed to be the best advice of the current experts. Just like past generations who used corporal punishment, which we now consider abhorrent, each successive generation learns from the mistakes of those before. Unfortunately, it's our children who have to grow through this learning process with the residual effects that last into adulthood.

The lesson learned is that praise needs to be earned and given in conjunction with the effort extended rather than from the outcome of that effort. A child with a reading disability may have to struggle to get through her homework, needing an enormous amount of encouragement and praise; whereas, another child may breeze through the same assignment in half the time with little required effort. Both may end up with the same grade, but the child who had to struggle needs more encouragement and deserves more praise.

Use the notion of doing one's best as a measure for your children's actions. Whether they did or did not accomplish their goal, ask them if they tried to do their best. If they say yes, believe them. Then be proud and pleased with their efforts even if you are disappointed in the outcome. Remind them that doing their best is all that counts. Be authentic in accepting their performance. If they did their best, even when you are not pleased with the end product, their best is all they can do! This is extremely challenging as a parent because, truthfully, most of us want our children to excel. We allow our own egos to define our expectations of them. There's no better example of this than when children are applying to college.

One of my son's high school friends was a great child and bright student. He applied to several respectable schools and got into most of them. Unfortunately, he didn't get into the one school his parents wanted him to attend. The reality of the situation was the school had over 20,000 applications for the limited 4,000 freshman spaces, so it was not his fault. However, they were so upset at his "failure," they punished him by taking his car keys away for a week!

One of the saddest parts of this story is that the parents couldn't celebrate and enjoy their child's accomplishment of getting into the many colleges that did accept him. How do you think this child felt going off to college? As a parent, you need to be aware of how to decipher your child's effort against the outcome. Often, these two may be out of sync because of something totally out of his or her control.

Taking responsibility for one's actions requires one to admit failure. It is the acceptance that not all that we do is going to be good. This is true for everyone. Accept the fact that both you and your child will make mistakes. However, teach her that being able to apologize and recover from those mistakes is what is important. Observing your mistakes will offer your child the freedom to make her own. Most importantly, this process will teach one of the most essential of all human traits: the ability to forgive.

Forgiveness

I can truly say I offered my boys plenty of opportunities to practice forgiveness from my many mistakes. I made one such honest mistake that resulted in the tragic death of my son Jake's pet rabbit. For four years, after my divorce, I lived with my boys in my parent's home. When Jake was in second grade, he begged to get a pet rabbit that my mother agreed to allow, as long as we kept it in the garage or outside. It had been a rainy, cold spring and finally the sun came out. I felt so bad that the rabbit had been stuck inside the cold, dark garage that I was excited to be able to give him some fresh air and sunshine. I pulled out his cage onto the driveway and went off to work.

When I arrived home from work, my mother came running up to my car. "We have a problem," she stated with a look of concern. She went on to say that she was doing her gardening when the rabbit gasped for air and fell over, dead, apparently, from heat stroke. In all sincerity, I had no idea that a rabbit couldn't be in direct sunlight. I knew they lived outdoors and thought the sun was exactly what he would enjoy.

My ignorance didn't help the fact I had to tell my son his rabbit had died and I indirectly killed it. Taking on that responsibility left me sick to my stomach for the three long hours before he came home from school and I had to break the news. I even thought about trying to switch the dead rabbit with a new one to avoid the inevitable, but didn't think I could pull it off. When Jake arrived home, I told him what happened and apologized profusely. After the look of shock and tears were wiped off his face, we found a box from his Papa's new golf shoes, lined it with soft material and had a formal burial.

They say that everything happens for a reason. This event taught Jake that I was capable of making big mistakes but it also taught him that I was able to apologize. Most importantly it gave Jake the opportunity to practice forgiveness. We replaced the rabbit with a pet hamster that could live in his room, under his control, and we moved on. Forgiveness, compassion and acceptance are all qualities we need to experience and practice before we can offer them to others.

Teaching One's Best

Teaching the concept of doing one's best to your children will be offering them an appreciation for other people's innate abilities and limitations. Accepting others for who they are with respect and dignity despite their physical or emotional limitations is an essential first step in your child being able to understand unconditional love.

One way to teach the idea of trying one's best while also teaching about limitations is to set up a few situations that ask your child to accomplish a relatively simple task but with an imposed limitation. For example, you can begin a discussion about always trying to do your best and how this means different things to different people. Suggest that at dinner you are gong to play a game. You are going to have her eat her dinner while blindfolded. This will give her an appreciation of how difficult it is for a blind person to do something she normally does with ease. All you will need is a long scarf, stretch headband or piece of fabric to tie around her eyes. Make sure it's tight so she can't peek. Then serve dinner as usual.

Ask her to try to do as much by herself as possible. You will gain a lot of information about her problem-solving style through observation. See how she goes about deciphering what is on the table. Does she figure out how to serve herself or ask for your help? Is she able to cut up her food? How can she pour herself a drink? All of these simple tasks will offer her an appreciation of how difficult it is for a blind person to accomplish what she takes for granted.

You can create other situations that impose a physical limitation such as strapping one arm to her side with a belt and ask her to do her homework or cover one eye and have her try to read a book. You can purchase wax earplugs used for swimming aids that will drastically alter her hearing and then have her listen to the TV or music or try to repeat what you say. There are many ways in which you can create situations that will teach her about her physical gifts that allow her to do things more easily than those without those physical attributes. As always, follow up these activities with a discussion. Talk about why we can't judge whether others did their best or not, unless we appreciate their effort. Discuss how this is difficult to see. Some people have physical limitations that are easier to see, but what about others who are mentally impaired or have emotional issues? Ask her how she feels about those who seem lazy and don't try. Follow up by reinforcing that if she always tries her best, she will never have any regrets since her best is all she can ask herself to do.

Self-Motivating Your Personal Best

An important question is how do we, as parents, instill internal motivation without our children depending on external reinforcement? One answer is to guide them to do what they love. Passion and effort will reward them with success because they will love the process of doing what they do.

The best way to accomplish this is to help your child discover her life's purpose. Take the time to watch for signs. Young children provide us with signs about what intrigues them all the time. It is our responsibility to notice the signs and encourage their interests even if they are not the same as our own. Observe and question what they do well. What do they continually choose to do? Is your child always in motion? Perhaps that is a sign that they are kinetically gifted. Is she always coloring? Then perhaps she sees the world through artistic eyes. Does she seem obsessed with animals? Maybe she might want to be a naturalist. All behavior emanates from a thought. Your child's behavior is physically offering you information as to how her mind works.

One of the most loving stories of encouragement I ever heard was from a mother who told me how she encouraged her son's passion for bugs despite the fact she despised them. She said that when he was a little boy, he was forever finding bugs and bringing them home stuffed into his pockets. This meant that every time she did the laundry and reached inside a pocket to check it for contents, she'd pull out some gross-looking insect. Despite her disgust, she never scolded him or discouraged him from his bug fascination. Today, he is studying the HIV virus, one could argue, a form of a bug, at Harvard Medical School. She told me she felt that by supporting his passion all of those years, she guided him into doing what he was passionate about.

There is a universal principle that says we are all placed on this earth, in this lifetime, to fulfill a specific purpose. Many adults weren't offered the opportunity to follow and develop their passions as children. As a result, they are now tirelessly working at jobs they don't like trying to fill a sense of emptiness by satisfying themselves with material things. The problem is that external satisfaction is only temporary.

Being able to live out your life's passion fuels one's existence from the inside out. Marianne Williamson wrote in her book, *A Return to Love*, "Everything we do is infused with the energy with which we do it." If you are angry and resentful about having to do a job each day that you hate, then that will be reflected into your performance. However, if a co-worker approaches the same job with an attitude of appreciation and enthusiasm, I guarantee that her performance will not only be superior, but others in the workspace will also feel her exuberance. Confucius wrote, "Choose a job you love, and you will never have to work a day in your life."

Take a minute and ask yourself what you feel passionate about. Maybe it's cooking; maybe it's watching your favorite sports team or gardening? It doesn't matter what it is. What matters is your child is able to observe you enjoying what you love to do. If you display passion and enthusiasm in your activities, your children will emulate this behavior.

Imagination: The Key to Finding Passion

The first step to accomplishing something is imagining that you can. Imagination is a form of thought. Einstein wrote, "Imagination is more important than knowledge." Imagination creates dreams to be realized. It offers a child to ask questions like "What do I want to be when I grow up?" or "What do I want to do with my life?" If a child thinks it, they believe they can become it. Remember the book *The Little Engine That Could*, by Watty Piper? It was the train's belief that he could go over the mountain that pressed him on to be able to do it. Often, it is usually an adult who extinguishes a child's dream by exposing the numerous obstacles that will be in the way of achieving success. Often our own fear of failure transcends to our children, and limits their belief in themselves.

We all hear of stories about children who defied the odds such as the homeless girl, Khadijah, who grew up on skid row and in homeless shelters. Khadijah believed that her only way out of the life she was born into was through education. With her vision, determination and hard work, Khadijah made it into Harvard University. The first step for Khadijah in accomplishing this enormous goal was to imagine it was possible. The belief that she could realize her dream, along with an amazing amount of passion and effort, allowed Khadijah to see her dream realized. "If you can focus your attention on giving your best effort to every task, the universe will sense your enthusiasm and readiness and open more doors to opportunities for you. Your confidence and enthusiasm are like magnets drawing more of what you want into your life." (Daily Om, 2010)

Encourage Imagination to Foster Dreams

Walt Disney wrote, "All our dreams can come true, if we have the courage to pursue them." Instilling courage in our children to pursue their dreams will come from an environment that encourages taking risks and sees challenges as opportunities rather than difficulties to be avoided.

Imaginative play is how children incorporate roles, test out hypotheses and become proficient at tasks. Henry David Thoreau wrote, "This world is but a canvas to our imaginations." This is particularly true for children. However, in order to imagine, children need time. Time to play. Time to experiment and test out their ability to impact their world. Play has been defined as a child's work. If a child is continually raced from one organized activity to another she will never have time to discover the mysteries that intrigue her or ideas that spark her imagination. This poem by Dr. Bruce D. Perry describes the magical cycle of how having the opportunity for exploration effects a child's development.

Self-Esteem

Curiosity results in Exploration
Exploration results in Discovery
Discovery results in Pleasure
Pleasure results in Repetition
Repetition results in Mastery
Mastery results in New Skills
New Skills lead to Confidence
Confidence contributes to Self-Esteem
Self-esteem increases sense of security
Security results in More Exploration

The first way to encourage imagination is by providing your young child time to explore her environment. Even before language develops, children are able to practice roles they have observed. In my classroom, I observed an 18-month-old holding a baby doll up to her breast pretending to feed it. She was obviously playing out, through imitation, what she observed her mom doing for her younger sibling. In another class, a couple of two-year-olds were "fixing" every nut, bolt and door jam they could find that was "broken" in our classroom with a toy drill and saw. I have also observed both boys and girls, as young as 15 months, sitting at a toy vanity putting on pretend lipstick and nail polish.

Young children need very little to amuse themselves. I have seen babies stare up at a revolving ceiling fan in amazement for an entire hour-long class. Many parents joke about the fact that children like the big box as much as they enjoy the toy inside. The fact is that it's true!

I would encourage you to find a big cardboard box. If you have older children, allow them to decorate it and turn it into anything they want. The little ones will follow along. It can be a fort, a hospital, a school: whatever they wish. My boys used to get so embarrassed because I would stop for any appliance box I would spot on the roadside in someone's trash. If that idea is beyond your comprehension, then you can call a store that sells appliances. They most often have to break down the large boxes the items come in and are more than willing to give one away, to get rid of it.

For slightly older children, instead of purchasing expensive battery toys that offer a predictable outcome when a specific button is pushed, or expensive video or computer games, I suggest going to your nearest thrift store. You will be able to find all types of inexpensive items that will challenge a child's imagination. You will most definitely find clothes that can be cut down to a child's size and be used as dress-up clothes. The quality will be better than the manufactured dress-up outfits that are made cheaply and cost twice as much. You can also find high heels, jewelry, hats and other items that can be easily washed and cleaned, ready to use in an imaginary dress-up play area. Even if you have to dry clean some items, it will still cost less than the poor-quality dress-up clothes you'll find in a toy shop.

The treasures in a thrift store don't have to be limited to clothing. One year, for the holidays, I purchased each one of my boys a large box radio and a screwdriver at the thrift store. The total purchase for both radios was six dollars. The screwdrivers were two dollars each. I wrapped up the radios and attached the screwdriver to the top of the box. When they opened up the box they had a stunned look on their faces. They had no clue what they were supposed to do with these old radios that they didn't ask for or necessarily want. I excitedly told them the radios were not for listening. Instead, they could take it apart to see how it worked and what was inside. The two of them furiously began to unscrew all of the screws they could find. It took quite a while and a lot of patience. It certainly captured their attention a lot longer than any other of their more expensive gifts. They couldn't wait until they could finally get inside. The radios were never intended to be used. Instead, I wanted to promote their curiosity, challenge their fine motor skills, and spark their understanding of how things work. It was the least expensive and most talked about gift of the season!

There are numerous ways to foster imagination in children that will help support their dreams. For example, if your child says she wants to be a movie star when she grows up, first ask her what that means to her. This way, you will have a better understanding of what image she has in her mind. If it is to wear fancy clothes, then let her dress up as a "movie star." You can take her picture and put it up on her mirror with some words like "This is me as a movie star." This may be all that she thinks about when she says she wants to be a movie star at her given age.

If she describes to you that she wants to act out a role, then you can begin by having her practice various facial expressions. Have her write out a variety of emotions on individual index cards or separate pieces of paper. Some suggestions are *happy, angry, scared, surprised, silly* or *nervous*. Have her sit in front of a mirror and pick a word from the deck of cards. Next, demonstrate how she can change her expressions depending on the word she chooses. After practicing this for a while, you can take it a step further by having her make the face and you try to guess what word she is acting out. Not only will this encourage her acting, but it will also help her to express emotions.

Taking it a bit further, the two of you can write a small skit together. Have her act out one of the parts. You can even videotape her and let her watch herself. If you want to take it even further you can invite siblings or friends to join in. You can present a show and invite guests, design tickets, create a playbill and make a set. The possibilities are endless. Your involvement can be as much or as little as you want, or as you are needed, with younger children requiring more direction.

Your child will most likely aspire to be a dozen or more different careers before she goes off to high school. As Mark Twain wrote, "They did not know it was impossible, so they did it." Encourage her to listen to her instincts that guide and direct her and most importantly, to follow her joy! As a parent, it is your role to observe and listen to the clues she is giving you and to nurture her talent and ambition. You never know which interest may end up being the right fit that will shape her life. With support, she will become whomever she envisions herself to be, no matter how difficult the goal feels to you. If she is encouraged to discover and follow her passion, you will be offering her a chance to live a life filled with joy, with a great chance for success.

Our personal dreams or desires can be called God's gift, our life's purpose or even our life source. Passion is an invisible energy within our heart and soul that motivates us to create visible effects. According to Kevin Hall in his book, *Aspire,* the true meaning of the word passion is "being willing to suffer for what you love. When we discover what we are willing to pay a price for, we discover our life's mission and purpose." This un-limited energy to persevere and perfect at all costs is what is often needed to give birth to our passion. It can create beauti-ful art or music, a new invention or a star athlete.

As a young adolescent, my passion was gymnastics. The desire to excel and master difficult skills drove me to train twenty-five plus hours a week and give up any semblance of a normal high school experience or social life. From most ev-eryone's perspective, it appeared like an enormous amount of hard work and sacrifice. For me it was like water for a thirsty animal; I couldn't get enough. When you experience that type of mindset, even if you are mentally or physically exhausted, then you know you are living your passion and on the way to realizing your dreams.

How many adults of past generations have had the op-portunity to recognize and develop this part of themselves? When we tried, how many of us were discouraged and told our ambitions were impossible? You might have heard, "You won't make money at it" or "It's not respectable" or most often it might have been implied that "It's not what I want for you as my child." Parents who had different intentions for many of us than we did for ourselves extinguished our dreams.

Too often we define success in our Western culture as those who have accumulated the most wealth and material things. Many of you might have seen the bumper sticker that reads, "Whoever has the most toys wins." This philosophy of life doesn't acknowledge the importance to experience joy in the process of doing. This poem by *Chuang Tzu* who lived 300 BC reflects this idea with reference to the art of target shooting.

The Archer

> When an archer is shooting for nothing he has all his skill.
> If he shoots for a brass buckle he is already nervous.
> If he shoots for a prize of gold
> he goes blind
> or sees two targets
> - he is out of his mind!
>
> His skill has not changed. But the prize
> divides him. He cares.
> He thinks more of winning than of shooting
> and the need to win
> drains him of power.

In other words, being focused on the goal can actually limit our skills because it takes our attention away from the process of what we are trying to accomplish. True passion will fuel itself from the doing, not from achieving. Working solely for the reward only acknowledges the effort once something has been achieved. That attitude is backwards. It's the process that should bring you the most joy, not the projected outcome.

Unfortunately, this competitive, materialistic approach to life has created many adults with an abundance of "toys" but too stressed and unhappy to truly enjoy them. Did you know that the word *stress* was first used to describe the malfunction of machines, not people! Yet, most adults live in a state of continual stress creating all kinds of health issues. Most often this stress can be attributed to their lack of enthusiasm for what they wake up to do everyday of their lives. It's a vicious circle. In order to buy all the stuff they think they need to make them happy, they have to work at a job they dislike that creates more stress.

It's important to ask yourself if you consider your life to be successful. Have you accomplished your dreams, or are you at least in pursuit of them? If not, why? Was there someone along the way that limited your belief in yourself? Did a teacher or parent discourage you from your career of choice? If achieving material success has been your ambition, are you ever sated?

These are difficult questions. Hopefully, your honest answers will offer you awareness into your personal motivations while reminding you to not limit your own children with your ego. Children will naturally believe in their unlimited potential. They will need you for support, encouragement and unconditional love along the way to realizing their dreams.

Being one's best is a philosophy that requires acceptance. Model the best attributes you hope to instill in your children through the synchrony of your actions and words. Then, believe that your child will do the same. Reward them for their efforts and motivate them to strive to pursue their dreams. Most importantly, demonstrate patience as they navigate their personal journey and forgive them for their failures. Parenting from your best means placing your focus on nurturing your child's dreams, spirit and heart.

CHAPTER 16

ROLE MODELING
YOUR PERSONAL BEST

"The most powerful moral influence is example."
HUSTON SMITH

Modeling appropriate behavior is a way to inspire our children through our actions. Very young children learn everything they know about their world through their five senses. They observe, listen and explore forming their understanding of how things go together and work. For years parents have been saying in jest, "Do as I say, not as I do" with the hope that their words had more effect than their actions. Talk about sending mixed messages to a young child.

Your words and actions need to be in synchrony or else you are living as a hypocrite. Remember, children are always watching and listening. Have no doubt that they are listening even while playing video games or watching their favorite show. They may not come when called for dinner, but they will know exactly what you said if it was something negative about their father or friend.

In the past, modeling has been defined as "setting the right example." Modeling a strong work ethic, cleanliness, respect for rules and regulations are some of the things you are being observed doing on a daily basis. However, it is most important to role model the invisible character traits we want to instill within our children. Things like good manners need to be observed by you using them. If we want our children to grow to become compassionate, caring adults, then you need to model concern, respect, compassion and empathy for others through your actions and conversations. Remember, doing leads to understanding and actions speak louder than words.

This is a sweet story of how a very young child is influenced and formed by modeling a parent's behavior.

Teaching Empathy

I currently teach over 75 children and their mothers weekly in my mommy and me program. Blessed by good health, it is quite rare that I ever miss a scheduled class. I know the children are expecting me to be there and I take their expectation very seriously. I don't want to disappoint them. This past year, however, I missed a full week of classes because I was recovering from surgery. The following week, I returned to class to be present and visible so as not to disappoint the children again.

As I stood by the door to welcome the children into the room, one of the moms was so excited to see me. While holding her son, Jamie, she said, "Look Jamie, Marcie is back. Marcie is all better." She then went on to tell me how upset Jamie was that I was "sick" and not able to be in class the prior week. She continued to say that every day since, he would frequently come up to her and ask, "Marcie sick?" She conveyed to me that he was clearly upset by my illness and needed continued reassurance that I was okay.

That day, I wasn't actively teaching, so I planted myself in a corner seat to observe the class activities while a substitute teacher assisted my co-teacher. Anyone who knows me knows that sitting still in one place is not my norm, especially in the classroom. Jamie kept looking over at me as if to make sure I was really there. His mother kept explaining to him, as he continued to check on me, that I was "all better." Every time he looked back at me, I blew him a kiss. He needed all those sweet check-ins to reassure him that I was really "all better."

I left the class amazed by the fact that here was a 20-month-old expressing real empathy and concern. It's hard enough for adults to show true compassion, never mind an almost two year old. I was so impressed with this little guy that I came home and told my husband.

The following week, I was back teaching at full capacity. When Jamie walked in, once again, he needed reassurance from both his mother and me that "Marcie was all better." We continued through our free playtime and then came clean up. In my program, everything gets put away before circle time so there are no distractions for the tender temperament and short attention span of the toddlers. As I was cleaning up, I attempted to push the Little Tikes kitchen into the closet. Jamie's mother immediately came over and said, "Don't do that. I'll get it for you." I was a bit surprised and a little overcome by her concern. I thanked her and began to lift up the driving bench to put that away and there she was again saying, "Marcie, let me do that. You need to take it easy." Once again I surrendered to her offer because I knew she was right.

Since my return after the surgery, many of the mothers expressed genuine concern for me by politely asking how I was doing. However, she was the only mother out of the 75 that went out of her way to help me, showing respect and compassion for me as a human being who had just undergone major surgery. It was an action her son was able to see and hear. At the time, I was a little humbled because she was right. In no way was I supposed to be lifting things thinking I could. It was so sweet and made me feel like I was more than just a paid professional.

Later in the week, I was talking once again about Jamie and his ability to be empathetic at 20 months when it dawned on me and the connection became clear. Jamie was the son of the only mother who went out of her way to make my life a little easier after my surgery. She not only expressed concern but she acted on it, serving as a role model for her son. Of course it made sense. The little boy, who knew how to have compassion and empathy, for another, had a mother who was capable of the same!

What a wonderful gift to be able to give our children -- to teach them by doing. They are constantly observing and listening to everything we say and do. If we want our children to grow into compassionate and empathetic adults, we need to model those attributes in our own lives. Saying kind words to others in front of your child is planting the seed and performing kind actions is allowing your child to watch those seeds bloom. Make a conscious choice to model concern for family, neighbors and strangers. Your children will follow suit. Teach your children that when they share, not only their things, but their time and energy, good will come back to them through joy.

This is a wonderful poem that exemplifies that our children are like sponges, ready to absorb all that we have to model and teach.

Children Learn What They Live
Dorothy Law Nolte, Ph.D.

If children live with criticism, they learn to condemn.
If children live with hostility, they learn to fight.

If children live with fear, they learn to be apprehensive.
If children live with pity, they learn to feel sorry for themselves.
If children live with ridicule, they learn to feel shy.
If children live with jealousy, they learn to feel envy.
If children live with shame, they learn to feel guilty.
If children live with encouragement, they learn confidence.
If children live with tolerance, they learn patience.
If children live with praise, they learn appreciation.
If children live with acceptance, they learn to love.
If children live with approval, they learn to like themselves.
If children live with recognition, they learn it is good to have a goal.
If children live with sharing, they learn generosity.
If children live with honesty, they learn truthfulness.
If children live with fairness, they learn justice.
If children live with kindness and consideration, they learn respect.
If children live with security, they learn to have faith in themselves and in those   about them.
If children live with friendliness, they learn the world is a nice place in which to live.

I would like to add one more: If children live with empathy, they will grow to understand their feelings and respect those of others. Stephen R. Covey in his book, *Aspire* wrote, "Empathy is to the heart what air is to the body." By modeling empathy, children will learn that we all have similar emotions and despite our differences, we all belong to the same species of humans. Ultimately, this will lead to the understanding that we are all connected. Hopefully, this awareness will grow to mean that it is important to nurture others and ourselves so that we can all thrive to live with respect in peace and joy.

This may seem like an infinitesimal goal. But imagine if every parent role modeled this type of cohesive behavior as the norm? It would become a way of living in this world for the next generation. That is what modeling is all about. We wouldn't need a natural disaster in order for us to reach into our pockets. Our older neighbor wouldn't have to be dying of cancer before we call to ask if she needs anything at the market because we are going anyway. We would live our lives in kindness rather than having to be reminded to practice random acts of kindness.

Today, most adults and teens live with the attitude that the world is a cutthroat, competitive place. Others are often seen as presenting a risk, upsetting one's personal agenda and being an obstacle to achieving individual goals. Life is experienced as a competition with the accomplishment of the goal as essential even if it is at the expense of another. This type of self-centered competitive behavior produces tunnel vision, greed and intolerance for the natural evolvement of things to happen and, of course, lots of stress.

Your child may be the first to read in her preschool class, but is she liked? Is she kind? Is she loving? Does she display respect and good manners? Or is she spoiled, selfish and full of her own ego? Lama Zopa Rinpoche, a revered Buddhist teacher describes "six perfections." They are *generosity, patience, morality, enthusiasm, concentration* and *wisdom*. I ask you to contemplate these virtues and that of compassion and kindness for a moment. How do you model these to your children? Your child may observe you living these on a daily basis, but to understand and incorporate them into her life, she must experience them for herself. One way to teach these valuable attributes is by doing. As a family, create situations where you are able to practice the philosophy of service to others.

Activities to Foster Compassion

Helping others is a natural way to feel good about oneself. Even very young children love to be helpers. During cleanup time in my classroom, children as young as 18 months can be seen carrying small buckets of toys into the closet in order to be a "big kid helper." They beam as they push toys the size of themselves into the storage room. Fostering the idea that everyone needs to cooperate and help will begin with your example and encouragement in the home.

Young children, once mobile, can begin to pick up their toys, carry small items into the house or go to get something at your request. All of these tasks also practice language development, listening skills and following directions. Once a child is a little older and is aware of colors, size, and the concept of same and different, they can help you with household chores that involve sorting. Give a young child the opportunity to help you sort socks; put away silverware from the dishwasher; or place clothes into the appropriate drawers. Through assigning family jobs, as children become more capable, they will learn and appreciate how families help to take care of each other. Have older siblings help younger ones with homework. This will take some pressure off of you and foster cooperation, patience and concentration. If a child displays a heightened interest on a specific topic, then make her the family expert on that subject. Children will love to teach you about what they learn and know. My youngest son is an expert on movies. He was always our "Siskel and Ebert" when it came to deciding on what movie to see.

The next step is to take this philosophy of helping others out into the community. What type of activity you do will depend of the age of your children. However, even a toddler can do her share and will learn through observation. Older children can participate in a discussion to help decide in what way you, as a family, choose to help others. There are many community-based volunteer activities that you can participate in such as cleaning up the environment, stocking a food pantry or handing out water at a road race. Often volunteer activities are listed in the local paper. You can also consult your library or religious facility for community needs. By visiting a food pantry to donate extra food or a shelter to donate outgrown toys or clothes, you will be giving your child the opportunity to practice generosity. A classic book about sharing and giving is *The Giving Tree* by Shel Silverstein.

You can also find local heroes in your community who have gone out of their way to help others and read about them with your children. Often senior centers or adult daycare facilities welcome the vibrant energy of children to brighten the day for their residents. You may bake cookies to deliver, draw pictures to hand out or sing a few songs. Whatever act of kindness you feel comfortable doing will most likely be greatly appreciated by those on the receiving end. Your children will benefit from the joy they experience in the moment and from the lifelong benefits that living a life full of compassion and service to others offers.

Teaching Compassion

Teaching your child compassion is to teach her to act from her heart for the sake of others. It requires expression and action. Some children have an innate sensitivity to other's suffering. In my class, I have witnessed how one child is injured and begins to cry, another child will be so upset at her crying that she will begin to cry too. However, understanding compassion comes from experiencing the painful events that life has to offer. As much as we want to protect our children from any pain, emotional or physical, we can't and we shouldn't. Life will surely show up in its many unexpected ways to teach this lesson. It is working through these painful experiences that allows us to create our emotional strength and build our ability to express compassion.

When I was eight, I had a pet cat named Smokey, who came limping home one morning dragging his tail. I remember his bone was exposed, covered in fur and blood. It was disgusting looking and I became hysterical. A car had struck him. My mother tried to soothe me and calm me down by promising to take him to the vet so he could "fix" him. I went off to camp in tears, tortured all day by the ruminating vision of his mangled tail.

Finally, camp was over and I ran into the house to find Smokey. My mother was on the phone and I had to wait for her to get off because I couldn't find him anywhere. I think she was probably gaining the courage to tell me that the vet had to put him down. When she finally told me, I began to sob, collapsing to the floor in anguish. No matter what my mother did, I was inconsolable. It was my first lesson in loss, experiencing the permanence of death. Finally she lost her patience and said, "See that's why you can't have any more pets. You get too attached and when they die it's too sad for you."

For years she held to her threat with me resenting her. In her desire to protect me from any more hurt, she inadvertently denied me the opportunity to practice recovering from the experiences of sadness, loss and responsibility that pets have to offer. She also conveyed to me that expressing my emotions of sadness was not okay and was punishable with severe consequences. Eventually, over the years, as I continued to beg, and she felt I grew to be able to handle it, she gave in and my siblings and I did get a variety of small pets as well as a few strays we managed to drag home.

Allowing children to experience life to its fullest will include uncomfortable or painful situations. Allowing them to express and navigate through all of their emotions, including the negative ones, will tear your heart apart and will teach them that they have the innate strength and capacity to endure all life has to offer. Compassion is the gift that arrives from experiencing a life lived. This is a beautiful poem by Naomi Shihab Nye that describes the process:

Kindness

Before you know what kindness really is
you must lose things,
feel the future dissolve in a moment
like salt in a weakened broth.
What you held in your hand,
what you counted and carefully saved,
all this must go so you know
how desolate the landscape can be
between the regions of kindness.
How you ride and ride
thinking the bus will never stop.
the passengers eating maize and chicken
will stare out the window forever.

Before you learn the tender gravity of kindness,
you must travel where the Indian in a white poncho
lies dead by the side of the road.
You must see how this could be you,
how he too was someone
who journeyed through the night with plans
and the simple breath that kept him alive.

Before you know kindness as the deepest thing inside,
you must know sorrow as the other deepest thing.
You must wake up with sorrow.
You must speak to it till your voice
catches the thread of all sorrows
and you see the size of the cloth.

Then it is only kindness that makes any sense any more,
only kindness that ties your shoes
and sends you out into the day to mail letters and
purchase bread,
only kindness that raises its head
from the crowd of the world to say
It is I you have been looking for,
and then goes with you everywhere
like a shadow or a friend.

Teaching Values

Before you can begin to teach your children values, it is essential for you to take an honest self-check about what is important to you. What motivates you in your life? What inspires you? Do you make comparisons between what you have and others have? How do you want to be remembered? What role does money play in your life? How important is it for you to be included with a specific group of people? Is it high up on your list of wants to be able to go to the hottest new restaurant or be able to wear the latest fashion? Is there an honor code by which you live all of the time or only when you are being observed? These are just a few questions that if you take a moment to contemplate, and answer honestly, might help you understand your own values since this is where your child's values originate.

Mahatma Gandhi wrote:

> "Your beliefs become your thoughts,
> Your thoughts become your words,
> Your words become your actions,
> Your actions become your habits,
> Your habits become your values,
> Your values become your destiny."

Your children are constantly observing and listening to your way of interacting in the world. They see how you treat others and hear your desires. They will learn to emulate and inherit your values as if by osmosis because they are immersed in your life, especially when they are young.

How do we raise our children to value what they have and inspire them to set goals for themselves without accumulating money as the sole reward? This is a really difficult task especially in our consumer-driven society. Over the past several years, young children have become the target consumer, marketed to through TV shows. Parents reinforce this type of marketing by buying the fad toys, sugary snacks and high-fat foods these shows promote because that's what their children are demanding and they don't want their children to feel deprived. As children branch out of the home, they become greatly influenced by the values of their peers. Therefore, your window of opportunity to be the only influence to instill strong family values is somewhat limited. So use your time well and begin young.

One thing is certain: The desire for material things complicates life. As John Gatto, New York City Teacher of the Year wrote, "Think of all the things that are killing us as a nation: drugs, brainless competition, recreational sex, the pornography of violence, gambling, alcohol and the worst pornography of all- lives devoted to buying things, accumulation as a religion."

Often the pressure to have "things" leaves us feeling inadequate if we can't provide what our children request or what we think we want for ourselves. This forces many of us to make choices that compromise our financial situation, leaving us in debt, laden with more stress. It becomes a vicious treadmill that is hard to escape once you allow yourself to jump on. If you feel like you have been pulled into this cycle, then ask yourself *why*? Are you buying your children things because you feel guilty about not spending enough quality time with them? Is it because you don't want them to feel different or left out? David Elkind wrote in The Power of Play, that "An unintentional consequence of using toys to promote social acceptance and positive self esteem is that it encourages conformity. Children come to see toys as vehicles of social acceptance rather than launching pads to imagination and fantasy. In addition toys are used as bragging points against children whose parents are less forthcoming."

Too many toys or things also make it harder to feel special about any specific one. Years ago, children received gifts at Christmas and on birthdays. Today, the pressure to buy toys is everywhere. Supermarkets, drugstores and even gas stations display toys in the most obvious places, deliberately tempting little eyes and hands. In order to not be pulled into the lifestyle of consumerism, you will need to consciously simplify your life. This is difficult to do. Ask yourself how much do you really need and how much do you actually have?

The first step in instilling values in your children is to establish your own unique family values. Culture, religion, or finances may influence what is important for your family. Whatever your personal values, it is important to have integrity and stand by what you believe, even when your child challenges you. This will require you and your partner to be in agreement of those values. The last thing you want is to say "no" and for your partner to say "yes" to the same request.

Instill in your children, from a young age, that love is energy. It is reciprocal and exists to be shared. Teach them that this is why toys and things are never totally satisfying. They can't love you back. Things may fill a void or an immediate desire on a temporary basis. But, explain to them that fairly quickly, they will come down from the excitement high of having something new and then want something else. Find a specific example of this to which your children can relate. I am sure there is something you bought that they begged you for or had a tantrum over that they no longer care about. This will bring your point across in a concrete, personal way. Things multiply creating clutter, which creates an unhealthy energy flow in your home, because they break and create the need for more things. Be determined not to allow your children to become a consumer addict. Try to take pleasure from what you possess without being attached to these things.

Memory Making

Try to live a family philosophy not driven by consumerism by setting the goal to create family memories instead of buying material things. Memories originate from the different or unexpected. They tend to conjure up emotions that we associate with the special situation we are recalling. One of my sweetest memories of when I was a child occurred when I was five. It was November 9, 1965, the date of the biggest blackout in history with several million people in the Northeast being left without power for up to 12 hours. My mother was preparing dinner at around 5 pm when it happened. I remember watching TV and it suddenly went black. Later that night, my mother piled my two siblings and me into her king size bed. There, she read us storybooks by flashlight until we fell asleep. I remember the event because of the togetherness I felt at the time. It was special to sleep in my mother's bed especially with my siblings. What I remember was the feeling of being safe, being part of a family and being loved. Think back on one of your favorite childhood memories and try to connect it with the feeling it brings up for you. That feeling you carry with you now, years later, is the gift you want to give your children. Not things.

Family Outings

If a child asks for a toy, you might say they can't have it because you are saving the money to go somewhere special on the weekend. During any family outing, make sure you take photos so you can look back together on the outing to enhance and reinforce the memories shared. Most children will not remember the expensive toy they received for Christmas, especially if it is just one of many they will get throughout the year, but they will remember the family outing where they went hiking and saw their first deer in the woods.

If money is an issue:

- Many libraries offer discount passes to museums and local popular attractions.
- Town parks usually offer guided family activities for little to minimal cost.
- Trails in public woodlands offer an opportunity for scavenger hunts, exercise and exploration. Bring along a notebook to jot down what you see or a paper bag to collect things. Older children might like to bring along a camera.
- Participate in a community event such as a cleanup day in a local park.

- Visit a nursing home or neighbor and deliver something special like cookies, magazines or drawings.

An Indoor Picnic

Some of the best memories you can create don't cost anything. You can use your own imagination to turn the same old routine into a special occasion. For example, instead of having dinner at the table one night, make a picnic on the floor. Begin by spreading out a blanket. Use paper plates and plastic forks just as if you were on a picnic outside. This will make the clean up easier for you. Some additional ideas are to print out some picnic type of scenes ahead of time such as a lake, mountains or a wooded park. Ask the children where they want their picnic to take place and then hang the photo on a wall above your blanket. While eating, you can pretend to be there. Start a story that will require everyone's participation such as, "I love our picnic up on top of this mountain. It was so hard climbing to the top it made me so hungry. I saw a moose on the way up. What did you see?" Maybe you can even wear your hiking boots, sunglasses or a backpack to the picnic just like you might do on a real hike. Prior to the picnic, you can go on a scavenger hunt and find some outdoor things you can bring indoors such as pinecones, leaves or small stones. You can also pretend to spray bug repellent on the children and even place a few plastic bugs on top of the blanket. Perhaps you might place your meal into a picnic basket to tote along. Afterwards, you can have the children draw a picture of all the things they "saw" on the hike and create a scrapbook. The activity is simple and inexpensive and the possibilities are endless, but the memory will be priceless.

Family Memory Board

What you will need:

- **Large bulletin board or wire rack**
- **Colored paper cut into approximately 1" x 10" strips**
- **Scissors**
- **Colored pencils, markers or pens**

Cut out several strips of paper and leave them in a bin near the bulletin board. Tell your children that any time they have a special memory they want to share or remember, they can write it onto a strip and tack it up onto the board. You might have to write it out for your younger children. Over time, the board will become quite colorful, decorated by lots of special memories.

If you have older children, and if you have access to a wire rack, you can also weave the memory strips through the rack to create a memory tapestry. If you do this, make sure you can still see what they wrote. The rack can even include three-dimensional objects they might find along the way that represent some special memory of an activity or event such as a ticket stub from a museum or a feather from a hike.

CHAPTER 17

THE VALUE OF APPRECIATION

*"Earth provides enough to satisfy every man's need,
but not every man's greed."*

MAHATMA GANDHI

Appreciation

Part of teaching values is to learn to appreciate what you have without always wanting more or better. Epictetus, a Greek philosopher wrote, "He is a wise man who does not grieve for the things which he has not, but rejoices for those which he has." This is difficult for anyone in our consumer-driven society, but especially for children who are bombarded with marketing campaigns targeted directly to _them_. Again, the example to simplify and do with less stuff needs to come from you. If you are always buying more and newer of the same things, like shoes, when you don't really need them, then you can't expect your children to think or want any differently when it comes to the things they like such as toys or video games. How many of us truly need everything we have in our closet?

If you are a parent of young children, then it will be easy to establish your philosophy about toys and gift giving early on and your child will expect this to be the norm. Regarding toys, more is most definitely not better and more expensive doesn't make it more educational or valuable.

Over the past few years, I have seen parents request "no gifts" on invitations to their child's birthday parties. This is a great idea that establishes a party as a time to share a special occasion with friends and not a time to reap in the loot. This eliminates the child being overwhelmed by numerous gifts at once. It also turns the focus for the child to appreciating her guests for their spending time with her and not for what the guests bring. Last, it eliminates the financial pressure that gift giving creates for your guests.

An alternative to gift giving for older children is to have them dedicate their birthday to a cause or charity. They can request that their guests make a small donation to a charity of their choice in honor of their birthday. On your invitation, suggest that your guests bring a food product you will donate to the local food pantry instead of a gift. Local libraries will also take book donations in honor of a special occasion.

By taking the focus off of the gifts and placing it on the people, your children will learn the joy of spending time with friends. Joseph Murphy wrote in *The Power of the Subconscious Mind,* "The real things of life, such as peace, harmony, integrity, security, and happiness, are intangible. They come from the deep self of human beings." Most importantly they will learn the value that true joy is in giving, not in receiving. You will also be teaching the universal law that states, "That which you seek is always found, and that which you give is always replenished."

If you have older children who are used to a traditional birthday, receiving numerous gifts from guests, and want to implement a change, then you will need to prepare them ahead of time to get used to the idea. They may view this change in philosophy as a punishment. I suggest you set the example first on your birthday. Tell them that this year you are very blessed and have everything you need; therefore, you don't want any presents. Explain that you have told family and friends who want to give you something, to make a donation in honor of your birthday. Also, elaborate on the fact that you are excited about celebrating the event with the people you love. Maybe this year, instead of a gift, you can do something special like go away for a weekend or eat dinner out at a favorite restaurant. This will set an example and reinforce the lesson of creating a memory rather than buying things.

I suggest you list all the things for which you feel grateful. This will show your children what is important to you. As an activity, ask them to do the same. See what they choose to write. This will offer you insight into whether they understand the message you are trying to convey. Follow up by planting the seed that when it is their birthday, the family will celebrate in a similar way when it comes to gift giving. You can decide how far you want to take this new idea. Maybe you will decide that your children should get a gift from you and grandparents but not their friends. Do what you feel comfortable doing, but place the emphasis on the celebration and not the gifts. This philosophy can also be extended to the exchange of holiday gifts.

Envy, the idea that you have what I want, and therefore I lack something, is a self-defeating attitude according to karmic principles. Children often express envy in wanting what their friend has, often just because the friend has it and they don't. Feeling envy will create resistance in being able to get what you want. This is because if you believe you lack something, you put the negative energy of "lack" out into the world and you will not be able to attract it to you. Instead, you need to be grateful for what you have and set forth the positive intention of creating more of what you want in your own life. Positive visualization, positive thoughts and effort will reward you with your intention.

If your child is demanding and she wants a specific thing like a new phone because hers isn't good enough and can't do everything that her friend's can, ask her to think of positive ways she can earn money to buy herself a new phone. Tell her to start by appreciating the phone she has. Remind her that many children don't have phones at all. One way to exemplify this is to say, "There will always be someone who has more than you and always someone who has less." This is an interesting idea that she most likely will appreciate and understand. If not, give an example like, you may live in a big house, but a princess lives in a castle and other children live in a hut without electricity or running water. Making comparisons that make sense will put her desires into perspective. This is especially critical if you live in an area where most children do have cell phones or other expensive items she wants. Next, have her visualize herself earning the money she needs to buy the phone. Maybe she sees herself babysitting, or washing cars or collecting cans. Have her set a positive goal. Maybe you offer to match it when she earns half of what she needs. Reinforce to her, especially if she gets discouraged, that being positive about her desire, rather than negative about her current situation will create the positive energy that will make her goal happen.

Greed, the intense and selfish desire for something, is a poison that has infested some of the brightest minds in heads of government, presidents of financial institutions and prominent members in the business community over the last several generations. These people have placed their own ambitions and greed ahead of the welfare of the whole.

Greed is the mindset of *I want more of what I want and I'll use my power and resources to get it despite whom I hurt or laws I have to break along the way.* Greed is ego driven. It's based in the belief of me, myself and I at the expense of others. It's the belief that the ends justify the means as long as I come out ahead.

The epitome of how greed can destroy is the story of the man named Bernard "Bernie" Madoff. He ran the largest Ponzi scheme in history, which existed over several decades. His fraud and lies caused the loss of billions of dollars to investors including charitable institutions, schools and religious organizations. He was arrested in December of 2008 for fraud, money laundering, perjury and other charges. Madoff received a 150-year prison sentence for his atrocious crimes against society. He is a perfect example you can use to educate your children about what *not* to emulate. One can only hope that this is just the beginning of his retribution and the karmic debt created by his selfish actions will follow him well into his next lifetime.

Teaching children to be aware of the consequences of their desires and behaviors, as it relates to others, begins in the family. Winston Churchill wrote, "There is no doubt that it is around the family and the home that all the greatest virtues, the most dominating virtues of human society, are created, strengthened and maintained." Your family is a microcosm of society, made up of individuals with different personalities, strengths, weaknesses and energies. Learning to accommodate those differences in others within the family will prepare them to identify, respect and get along with those outside of the family. Understanding how one member of the group affects the whole will reinforce the ideas of cause and effect and the karmic principles we discussed earlier.

Appreciating Abundance

What you will need:

- Small wooden treasure chest
- Assorted colored beads and jewels
- Markers or paint

This is a fun activity to do with more than one child since it will encourage sharing, the understanding of abundance and the karmic principle of we get back that which we give. If you are doing this activity with just one child, purchase two small wooden treasure boxes at a craft store, one for each of you. If several children are participating you will need one box for each child. Buy a variety of colored stones, jewels or beads so you have more than you will need to fill all of the boxes. This is an important way to demonstrate abundance visually. Place your treasure into a large container and mix the beads and stones thoroughly.

Explain to the children that we are lucky to have all that we need. Initiate a conversation about how some children experience a lack of things we take for granted such as running water and plenty of food. See if they can think of things of which they have plenty, whereas others may not.

Explain to the group that they can fill their treasure box with any of the beads and jewels they like. Once everyone is finished filling their treasure box explain that the box they made is not for them but for someone else. Observe their reactions. Are they gracious and excited about giving their treasure to someone else? Are they resentful about giving up what they thought was theirs? Remind them that everyone will still get a box and show them that there are still many more beads and jewels to choose from if they need to complete their treasure.

Have the children place all of the boxes into the center of the table. Have them close their eyes and mix them all up. Then allow each child to pick a box. Once they have chosen a box encourage them to decorate the outside any way they choose.

CHAPTER 18

Using the Invisible to Create our Experience

"The thing you set your mind on is the thing you ultimately become."

NATHANIEL HAWTHORNE

For most of us, the knowledge of how the Internet functions is a mystery. Yet, we are more than willing to use its resources without understanding the process of how it works. Tapping into the mystery of what the universe has provided for us follows the same principle. Energy and vibration may not always be visible but they exist and can be measured. We may not comprehend *how* miracles happen, but the fact exists that they do. People recover from terminal cancers; mothers perform heroic acts of strength to save their child's life; and people change their regular routines for no apparent reason which prevents them from being in harm's way. Albert Einstein wrote, " The most beautiful thing we can experience is the mysterious. It is the source of all true art and science."

In 2006, the book *The Secret* by Rhonda Byrne became a bestseller by suggesting that our thoughts create our perceptions, reality, and destiny. This seemingly "new age" notion that we have the ability to manifest all we desire within our subconscious mind, whether it be miracles of healing or the accumulation of wealth, is not new. In fact, the ancient Roman poet, Virgil, who lived from 70BC to 19AD wrote, **"**They can because they think they can."

The law of attraction as described in *The Secret* is, in fact, a concept that goes back all the way to ancient teachings. In the Bible from St. Matthew we are taught to believe, "Ask, and it shall be given you. Seek and ye shall find. Knock and it shall be opened unto you. For everyone that asketh, receiveth and he that seeketh, findeth and to him that knocketh, it shall be opened." The book *Thoughts are Things* by Prentice Mulford in 1889 explored the relationship between our "spiritual mind" and its effect on our life experience. "We have, through knowledge, the wonderful power of using or directing this force when we recognize it, and know that it exists so as to bring us health, happiness and eternal peace of mind."

Our words create our thoughts. They define how we see ourselves and offer a way to express those feelings out into the world. Thoughts establish our expectations and set in motion the life we choose to create for ourselves. This interplay between our thoughts and how we experience life is essential. It is the belief in your mind that creates the circumstances of your life. You create your thoughts and they create your reality.

The notion that we all hold the potential to create who we are and what we experience offers up many questions. If one has that capability then why would we choose to have pain, suffering, poverty and disappointment as part of our lives? The answer, according to the law of attraction, is that we actually do create most of our own chaos as a means of learning "life lessons" that will help us evolve to a higher spiritual self. In his book *The Power of Your Subconscious Mind,* Joseph Murphy wrote, "All your experiences, all your actions, and all the events and circumstances of your life are but the reflections and re-actions to your own thought." If this is so, then we can just as easily attract negative experiences through negative thoughts as we can positive ones.

Most of us deny this cause and effect connection between our thoughts and experiences because that would make us ac-countable. We would rather choose to accept what life seem-ingly hands us by taking on the "victim" role throughout our lives. It is easier to confront failure with blame than to think that we could have had a role in our own demise. By accepting the law of attraction we are accepting the responsibility for our own life path, both good and bad. Expanding our mind around the notion that we can have an impact on our own destiny by the thoughts we think is an amazing concept laden with re-sponsibility. This concept is based in the universal principle that like attracts like.

Explaining the Law of Attraction to your Children

I like to think of the law of attraction as the law of empow-erment for children. Can you imagine if you were taught at a young age that you create much of what you experience in your life? Life wouldn't feel so random and you would experience a sense of control towards situations that challenged you along the way. Buddha taught, "What we are today comes from our thoughts of yesterday, and our present thoughts build our life of tomorrow: our life is the creation of our mind."

You can simplify the concept of the law of attraction for your children by explaining that the thoughts and ideas within their heads are extremely important. Because even though other human beings can't read their thoughts, the universe can. The law of attraction states that we attract what we think about, so we want to be sure that we choose positive thoughts full of love, not fear or anger.

To begin to teach the concept of like attracting like, it is first important that your child understands the concepts of same and different. This is a developmental skill that usually develops around three years of age. Many educational stores sell card games picturing objects that fit into categories of same and different to teach this concept. If you do not have access to these, you can create your own cards.

Category Cards

What you will need:

- **Pictures of things you can categorize**
- **Scissors**
- **Card stock**
- **Glue**
- **Markers**
- **Clear contact or laminate**

Download or cut out pictures of objects from magazines that you can categorize into groups you would call the same or different. For example, people and animals; fruits and vegetables or cars and trucks. For older children, you can make the categories more subtle and difficult to sort such as mammals and reptiles; winter clothes and summer clothes or hard and soft.

Next, cut out several squares of card stock approximately 2 x 2 inches. Glue the pictures onto the cards. This is a fun art activity in which to have your child help if she is capable. Write each category onto a piece of card stock and place it beside the matching picture. If your child isn't a reader yet, then glue a picture next to the word that represents itself so she can make the association of the picture to the word. Shuffle the cards and ask your child to place the appropriate card under the correct label. This is a very visual and concrete way to demonstrate the idea of same and different.

Once you are sure your child understands this notion on a concrete level, you can begin to expand the idea of the law of attraction to include her thoughts. Begin by saying, "There is a law of the universe that says, 'Like attracts like.' It is one of the most powerful laws in the universe. You may even suggest that she has superpowers when it comes to what she thinks and how she feels. Explain that this law says she can bring into her life that which she thinks and believes. It is important to discuss that this means she has the ability to bring both good and bad into her life, so she should always be aware of how and why she is thinking certain things. Have her talk about some of her thoughts and the corresponding feelings that go with them.

One way to develop awareness of one's thoughts is learning how to identify, label, categorize and manipulate them. This is a great first step in understanding that we can control how and what we think.

Good Thought / Bad Thought Boxes

What you will need:

- **Two small boxes of similar size**
- **Glitter, markers, stickers**
- **Glue**

- **Brown paper, wrapping paper, fabric scraps and yarn**
- **Dirt or coffee grinds**
- **Scissors and paper**

This activity is meant to demonstrate to your child that only she has control over her thoughts. This is a difficult concept for adults to grasp so it's great to introduce this concept early. Practicing this exercise will make it believable to your child as she gains experience in recognizing, labeling and managing her thoughts. This is something adults continually strive towards.

The two boxes are meant to provide a concrete visual way to help her sort her thoughts into good and bad or positive and negative, building on the concept of opposites. If she is having a difficult time understanding your request, give her examples of varying type of thoughts. For example, "Sometimes I feel scared that I'll make a big mistake at work" or "I feel so excited and happy about going out with Daddy on Saturday night" or "I'm worried that I'll gain weight if I eat too much cake."

Explain to her that only she is in control of her thoughts. Discuss how she can be the "boss" of her thoughts. The first way to control your thoughts is to acknowledge that they exist. Sometimes they are hard to share with others. Tell her that one way to get rid of bad, scary or negative thoughts is to write them onto a piece of paper and throw them out of her mind into the negative thought box. On the other hand, talk about how her good, positive thoughts can help her and those are the thoughts she wants to keep.

Ask her to categorize her thoughts so she can practice the concept of good or bad thoughts. Show her the two boxes and tell her that you are going to make a box for all her bad thoughts and another for all her positive, good thoughts. Remind her that if she has a bad thought she can write it down and get it out of her mind by putting it into the box.

Bring out the two boxes and ask her to decorate them. You can suggest that the bad thought box may be covered in dirt, coffee grinds or black marker or any other way she experiences these bad thoughts. If you want to cover the negative box in dirt, first paint it with glue and then sprinkle the dirt over it either outside or over a waste bin. A good layer of dirt will stick to the glue and you can brush off the excess. Then, let her decorate the good thought box with beautiful things like colored paper and glitter. Once the boxes are decorated cut a slit into the top to resemble a mail slot.

Ask her to write out a thought onto a piece of paper and place it into the appropriate box. Tell her she can do this when she feels the need. Let her also know she can throw out the bad thoughts any time she wants.

Magnetic - Like Attracts Like

What you will need:

- **Strong magnet**
- **Magnetic objects that you can find around the house *or***
- **Magnetic tape that can be purchased inexpensively at craft stores**
- **Non-magnetic household items**
- **Marker**
- **Paper and scissors or self-adhesive labels**
- **Plastic tray or plate**

Reiterate that like attracts like. Explain that the magnet represents her thoughts and will stick to things like itself. Write "positive thoughts" on a label and stick it to the side of the magnet. For an older child you might be able to get away with just saying, "Imagine this magnet represents your thoughts." Next have her explore the different items and see which ones stick to the magnet. Explain that in order to stick to the magnet, they all have to have the same thing in common namely, iron. Show her how the magnet will not stick to the things that do not have iron, like a piece of plastic or paper.

If you have magnetic tape, cut a piece and stick it to one of the non-magnetic items that didn't stick before. Explain that if we change our thoughts like we changed the item, by placing the magnetic tape onto it, we can attract new things into our lives. To elaborate further on the idea that good thoughts create good experiences, you can create the following "Go-Fish" type of game.

Cause and Effects of Thoughts Fishing Game

What you will need:

- Strong hand held magnet (you can purchase this at an educational or hardware store)
- Strips of card stock cut out into the same size 1/2 inch by 5 inches
- Self-adhesive magnetic tape or paper clips
- The same number of 2 x 2 inch square cards as strips of paper
- Marker
- Scissors

(If you want to make a "fishing pole" you can attach your magnet to a string and tie the string to a small dowel, stick or ruler.)

On each 2 x 2 card, write out a thought. It is important to include both positive and negative thoughts. Then, on the long strip of paper, write out what that thought might attract. Place the magnetic adhesive onto the back of the longer strip. If you do not have this, then you can use paper clips. Punch the paper clip through the end of each of the longer strips. This is a great lesson in cause and effect, which you can also use when teaching about karma. Here are a few examples:

"I am afraid to try new things." on the 2 x 2 card.
On the strip of paper, write: *"**I am bored with always doing the same things.**"*

"I want to be a doctor."
On the strip of paper: " *I get accepted into medical school."*

"I am afraid of airplanes."
On the strip of paper: *"I never get to go to far away places."*

"I love flowers."
On the strip of paper: *"I am a great gardener and grow beautiful flowers."*

I would suggest letting your child guide you as to what she wants to write. However, if she is having difficulty with something specific, then I suggest writing that problem area out for her. This might be a good way for you to approach a difficult situation. Shuffle the square cards and divide them up between the players. Place all of the long strip pieces - the effect pieces - in a pile in the middle of the table or floor. Explain that the object of the game is to fish out the effect that the thought in her pile might have on someone's life. The idea is to match each thought to its corresponding effect. If you get the wrong effect, then you throw it back into the middle pile. You can place the effect pieces right side up or upside down depending on how you want to play the game. The first one to get all of their matches wins.

You can silly it up a bit by writing some random effects onto strips of paper like, "You grow a purple nose" or "You turn into a frog." Laughter creates a positive experience and positive experience is a great teacher.

CHAPTER 19

Affirmations and Manifesting Desires

"He is able ... who thinks he is able."

BUDDHA

Achieving one's goals is a long process that first begins with the thought, "I can." Stating affirmations is built on the premise discussed earlier, that our words create our thoughts and our thoughts create our experiences. Therefore, affirmations use positive "I" statements in the present tense that build confidence and self-esteem to help accomplish one's goal.

You can find several books about affirmations for children on www.amazon.com. Louise Hay wrote, *I Think I Am* that explains affirmations and how they work. Another is *Incredible You* by Dr. Wayne Dyer. You can introduce affirmations to your child through modeling positive language and affirmations about yourself. After offering your child some examples, see if she can add some positive "I" statements about herself. She may surprise you in how she sees herself. Keep it simple and fun. Here are a few examples that reinforce self-confidence:

"I believe in myself and my abilities."
"I am a fast learner."
I have many gifts and talents."

Later on as you become more comfortable and affirmations become a part of your routine, you can introduce some that might suggest to your child a change in behavior you would like to see. For example, "I am always on time." or "I love to share my things with my sister."

One way to bring affirmations into your life is to write positive statements onto pieces of paper and place them around the house. Start with simple statements like "I am happy" or "I am safe" or " I have lots of energy."

Affirmations can build confidence when said repeatedly. For example, maybe your child is having anxiety and doubt about her ability to get a good grade on her spelling test. What you can offer her is a short phrase such as, "I am great at spelling and know all my words." Write it on a piece of paper and stick it to her bedroom mirror where she will see it before she goes to school. Encourage her to silently say it to herself several times throughout the day. This will hopefully remind her to practice her words as well.

Affirmation Activities

There are a several creative ways you can keep track of your affirmations. Here are a few suggestions you can do together.

Affirmation Flip Cards

What you will need:

- **File cards or card stock**
- **Markers**
- **Metal rings**
- **Hole punch**
- **Clear contact paper**

Cut the card stock into 3 x 5 inch pieces. On the front of one side of the card, write down the affirmation. Use the back to decorate or express the affirmation. To preserve your cards, I suggest taking the time to either laminate them professionally or cover them in clear contact paper. After they are laminated, punch a whole into the top left and right corner and place a ring through each hole. By making two holes with two rings the cards should be able to stand up on a dresser or night table.

If your child is too young to read, write the affirmation on the front and make sure there is a picture on the back that represents the affirmation. She will be able to make the connection after a few times of practicing these together. Then this will also be a bit of a memory game.

My Affirmation Book

You can extend the above activity by actually creating an affirmation book with your child that represents all of her positive traits.

What you will need:

- **Any type of paper including plain white paper, construction paper, or card stock**
- **Markers**

- **Photographs**
- **Collage materials**

Decide how big and how long you want to make your book. You can fold an 8 1/2 x 11 sheet in half or keep it full size. If your child is young, I would recommend folding the paper in half so it will be easier for her to hold it herself. I suggest leaving some pages empty to be filled in at a later time when your child will most definitely come up with new affirmations about herself.

Explain to your child that this is a book all about her best self and the self she dreams to become. Begin by writing one affirmation on a side of paper. Then have her decorate the page with things that describe that affirmation.

For example, if she writes, "I believe I can be whatever I want to be," then have her draw a picture of what she wants to be when she grows up. If her goal is too hard to draw, download pictures to represent her affirmation. I suggest trying to come up with more creative ways to illustrate your book and use online artwork as a last resort.

A fun idea is to take pictures of your child acting out her affirmations. If she says, "I am super fast and can win races," then take a picture of her running and glue that to the back of the affirmation. Not every page has to have the same format. You might want to color some pages, use photos for others and collage for the cover. Most importantly this should be a creative project of self-expression.

Before putting the book together, I would recommend laminating the individual pages as long as there aren't three-dimensional objects decorating the pages. Once laminated, you can assemble it in a few simple ways.

Before assembling the pages decide if you want a cover. I would recommend making a cover so that it looks like a book. You can make a cover out of cardboard or card stock. Make sure you come up with a title. "The Best Parts of Me," "My Affirmation Book," or "Things I Believe" are just a few ideas. Have your child write her name as the author. Inside the cover you can write the date. This will be great to have when you look back at it years later.

Stack the pages on top of each other to give you the correct order you want to see. Try to leave a few blank pages at the end. Punch two holes on the left side. Place each hole approximately one inch from the top and bottom of the page. You can tie the book together with yarn or string or use metal, three-ring binders. You can purchase these inexpensively at a stationary store. Lastly, if you have put a lot of work into the book and would like to make it seem more like a real book, you can have it spiral bound at a copy center. This little book will become a treasure for the both of you as she grows older and looks back at her dreams, aspirations and self-concept at a particular age.

It is essential when teaching your child about affirmations that she understands this is just the first step in realizing her dream or desired goal. Thinking is only a first step. Her intention and attitude about going after her affirmation is a second step. But the third and most important step she needs to understand is that making dreams come true takes very hard work. No matter what book you read regarding the power of thoughts, it takes hard work and determination to manifest that thought out into the real world.

In Malcolm Gladwell's book *Outliers*, he discusses the ten-thousand hour rule that neurologist Daniel Levitin has found to be true through his research on individuals who have attained mastery in their field. "The emerging picture from such studies is that ten thousand hours of practice is required to achieve the level of mastery associated with being a world-class-expert at anything.... It seems that it takes the brain this long to assimilate all that it needs to know to achieve true mastery." This is why it is so critical for a child to be allowed to follow her passion. Ten thousand hours is an enormous amount of time to spend on becoming proficient at one skill. Practicing something you love is motivated by desire. Practicing something forced upon you is motivated by fear and threat of punishment.

Like many girls of my generation, I was introduced to dance classes when I was a child. It was the likely extra curricular choice for girls during those years since girls' team sports hadn't yet evolved. I intuitively managed to gravitate towards the acrobatic aspects of dance. I loved being upside down and flipping through the air. When I was around 12, I was introduced to gymnastics and fell in love. I began training several hours a day, five to six days per week as part of a small elite club that trained in the public schools after hours. Back in the early 1970's, gymnastic schools as we know them today didn't exist. As if the rigorous workouts weren't enough, any spare time I had I used to choreograph and practice balance beam routines in my family's formal living room that was normally "out of bounds." I say out of bounds because no one was allowed there except for company. However, my mother broke the rules and supported my passion by allowing me the opportunity to use the living room to practice since it offered a large open area. A few months later she gave in again. After much begging on my part, she allowed me to place masking tape on the carpet to resemble my imagined four-inch wide balance beam. I spent hours rehearsing skills within those strips of masking tape, motivated solely by my dreams of becoming a gold medalist. I needed no prodding other than my own burning desire to see my dream realized. Most often the only parental input I got came more as a threat to stop practicing. Admonitions came in the form of, "It was time to go to bed" or my mom would joke that I needed to stop because "I was going to wear out the rug." This passion and practice, combined with my vision of becoming a champion, earned me the Senior National Balance Beam title in 1976 and the balance beam gold medal in the 1977 Maccabiah games in Israel.

Realizing one's dream takes real work. It also takes supportive parents. My mother jokingly said that one of her happiest days was when I got my license and she didn't have to drive me to workouts at the gym any longer. She had been doing the hour-long, round-trip drive, six days a week for several years to make sure I got to and from practice on time. Your child's dreams, intentions and hard work will need your belief and support in order to even have a chance of being realized.

Practicing the Process of Manifesting

Along with hard work, manifesting a desired outcome of a particular thought is a process to be learned, practiced and most importantly to be believed. There are three steps to follow to facilitate this process:

1. You must set your intention with belief, conviction and passion.
2. You must state your intention in the present as if you already have it.
3. Your intention cannot be for your sole benefit alone. It must not be for selfish gain. This is particularly important if asking for something material like money.

Setting your intention, with belief, is the essential first step in manifesting the desired results of any thought. This entire process must be done with emotion and conviction. Idle thoughts will not yield results. It is not until we put emotion into our thoughts that they have energy to materialize into a reality. Maintaining pure belief is hard to do when everyday events continue to occur that seem to resist the notion of your desire being realized. In other words, it's not enough to just state your desire. It is more effective to believe it with your heart and soul.

For example, suppose you really desire to have a new house because you have outgrown your current home. You and your partner find a perfect house but it is currently more than you can afford. However, you can't get your mind and heart off of it. Using your imagination, begin to visualize yourself in it. Imagine yourself cooking dinner in the kitchen and your family sitting together around the table at a family meal in the dining room. See your children playing in the front yard while you work in the garden. Visualize yourself going through the front door and seeing how you might decorate the house. What pictures are on the walls? Inhale the smells that will fill the air. Hear the noise of your children's favorite TV show coming from the family room. See yourself having a place for all of your stuff neatly organized and put away! All of these visualizations will become more real to you as you allow yourself to experience the desire through your senses, feelings and emotions.

The second step is to ask for what you want as if you already have it in the present. This is an important karmic principle that is essential in manifesting your dreams. It's based in the idea that "If you seek something, it means you do not have it." It is expressed as a lack of the thing you desire and will prevent you from attaining it. Don't see the house as something you don't have now that may come in the future. Instead, experience it as if you already own it. This may sound like you are trying to fool yourself and the universe, but in reality, your dream house does already exist exactly as you see it to be -- in your mind. Remember: Our thoughts create our reality.

Now let the universe provide. You might begin to see things happening that will lead you towards accomplishing your dream. Perhaps you are offered a job promotion. Maybe you get a larger than expected tax refund. Maybe the price of the house is reduced. The important thing is to keep your belief, see the opportunities that come your way and strive through hard work to realize your goal.

Last, it is important to trust the universe. If for some reason that specific house doesn't materialize, then it wasn't meant to be. Have faith that a better one will become available to you down the road. Having faith is difficult to do when you are disappointed in the immediate response. But conviction behind your dream will facilitate the process of it becoming real.

With much attention and scientific discoveries regarding the effects that thoughts have on reality, it is worth the consideration, even in the most rigid of minds, that this phenomenon is feasible. Imagine the gift of empowerment you can give to your children by teaching such a concept to them when they are young. Inspirational author William Arthur Ward wrote, "If you can imagine it, you can achieve it; if you can dream it, you can become it." With this belief in the power of her thoughts, can you imagine how the world's possibilities would begin to open up for your child? When you ask your child, "What do you want to be when you grow up?" This question would invoke all the possibility that her imagination and desire could provide with the belief that she possesses the ability to make it happen.

Here is an example of how to use the process of affirmations to inspire your child's dreams and aspirations: Your child states that she wants to be an astronaut when she grows up. Now we all know that this is a big dream that will take education, physical stamina, timing and some luck to realize. Instead of allowing your own fear of trying to protect her from frustration or defeat surface, begin to visualize her potential and support her idea. You can say, "Wow that is really cool. What do you think you can do now that will help you to become an astronaut when you grow up?" See what she says. Then you can suggest writing on a piece of paper "I am a great astronaut and one day I am going to fly on a space mission." Have her post it on her mirror. Suggest you both get some books out of the library so she can read about famous astronauts. You can visit the science museum or a planetarium together. Supporting her dreams in any way will show her you trust in her abilities.

It is important to teach your child that the intention behind her thought is as equally important as the thought itself. For example, *"I want to have a lot of money to buy anything I want"* is a thought that might invoke a negative response from the universe since it is a thought of selfishness. Explain that most likely this thought won't create an abundance of money since her intention originated in selfishness. A better way to phrase the affirmation is, *"I have plenty of money in my life to buy all the things I desire and enough to contribute to those in need."* This will evoke a much more positive response from the universe.

Here is another example of a positive affirmation regarding co-creating with the universe. It's the idea I had about the process of turning the idea for this book into the reality of a book in print. I said the affirmation, *"I am a successful author and people love my book. I know I inspire young parents who will enlighten the next generation. I can make a difference using my God-given abilities."* That statement would be more proactive and more supported by the universe than stating, *"I want to be a successful author and sell a million copies of my book."*

Teaching the Importance of Thoughts

Thoughts are Like Seeds

What you will need:

- Small flower pot
- Flowering seeds
- Potting soil
- Large spoon
- Paper
- Scissors
- Markers

Begin by saying, "When you think a thought, it's like you are planting a seed for the thought to bloom out into the universe." Before anything can happen someone has to think of the thought inside her mind. A simple example for you to say to her is, "Sometimes when I watch TV, I think, I want a drink. Then, I think that if I want a drink I have to go into the kitchen. So off I go. If I didn't have the thought that I felt thirsty, I wouldn't have walked into the kitchen. So it's the thought that motivated me to get up and walk into the kitchen." This is a great example of cause and effect.

Ask her if she can think of a few examples of how her thoughts determine her actions. If not, offer her another example such as the innovative thoughts that create new inventions. Explain that before cars existed, someone had the idea of building one. First that person had to see the car in her mind's eye. This took imagination since it didn't exist yet and no one knew what a car looked like. Then maybe she drew it onto paper. Next she had to find the materials to build the car and then had to make sure it worked. You can also use an example relevant to her such as, "If I envision myself getting an 'A' on my next math test, then I need to study hard and pay attention in class to help accomplish this."

You can elaborate by saying that sometimes there is a short distance between our thoughts and the desired results, and other times it can take years to accomplish our dreams. The important thing is to believe in what you want with all of your heart and then work very hard at making it happen. Now you can begin the activity.

You will need to purchase a small flowerpot, potting soil and seeds ahead of time. Have your child write a thought or an intention that she would like to make happen onto the paper and cut it into a thin strip that will fit inside the bottom of the pot. Fill the pot half way with dirt and plant a seed into the dirt. Have your child water and "nurture" the seed and explain that flowers take love, time, patience and effort to grow. They also need things that the universe provides like water, sunshine and air. Tell your child that her thought will also take time, hard work, her positive intention and the cooperation of the universe in order for her thought to manifest itself. A simple board book that exemplifies the concept of positive intention is *The Carrot Seed* by Ruth Krauss and Crockett Johns. It's a classic book that your preschoolers will enjoy.

Play Dough

Play Dough is another great way of demonstrating how our thoughts can create something that didn't exist before we thought of it. Below is a great homemade recipe that has been well tested over the last 30 years in my classroom.

What you will need:

(This recipe is designed to be cooked so you will need a stove and a pot.)

- **1 cup of flour**
- **1 cup of water**
- **1/2 cup salt**
- **1 tbs. oil**
- **2 Tsp of cream of tarter**
- **Food coloring**
- **Extract for a nice scent (I like to match the scent with the color. Strawberry for red, lemon for yellow, mint for green.)**

After having made this recipe hundreds of times, there are a few secrets to having it come out perfectly. Mix the food coloring into your water. This way the color will be evenly dispersed. I recommend the gel food coloring that is used for cake decorating, available in a craft store. The colors are more vibrant than the liquid food coloring you can get in the baking section of the market.

Mix all of the ingredients directly into the pot and cook over medium heat. As soon as the ingredients begin to congeal, turn off your heat and allow the heat to finish cooking the dough. If you cook the mixture too long, it will be crumbly. If you don't cook it long enough it will be sticky. It might take a couple of tries to get the texture just right. Store the dough inside a sealed plastic bag. It does not need to be refrigerated and will last at least a month or more.

You can use several kitchen utensils and items to work with the dough. Plastic swizzle sticks, cut-up plastic straws, colored toothpicks are all things your child can poke into the dough to create a sculpture. Cheese spreaders are a safe way she can

practice cutting the dough. Other ideas are to use cookie cutters, rolling pins, toy hammers, small cars to make tracks, or
plastic lids to make circles.

Older children will love Play Dough. It can be quite relaxing,
especially if you use it warm. Often mothers in my classroom
will be chatting at the dough table as they make up creations
even though their child has left to go off in a different direction. Besides alleviating stress, Play Dough offers a child the
opportunity to experiment without judgment. If she doesn't
like what she makes, she can just squish it down flat and start
again.

To tie this activity into the lesson of how thoughts become
things, you might play a guessing game with your child. Suggest that she think of something she wants to create with the
dough. Tell her not to tell you what it is. When she is finished
with her creation you can guess what she was thinking. Then
you can have a turn. You can name this game the "Mind Reader
Game."

Mantras as Affirmations

The word *mantra* is defined by breaking down the word
into two parts. *'Man'* means mind and *'tra'* means release. Mantras originated in the Vedic period thousands of years ago and
are usually chanted in Sanskrit but don't need to be. They are
associated with Hinduism. If you have ever chanted *"Om"* in
a yoga class, this is Sanskrit and a form of a mantra. Mantras
are considered to be a type of prayer that when repeated with
focus and belief awaken a higher consciousness producing a
desired effect. Quite often, mantras are repeated 108 times
using Mala beads to keep track of the recitations. The reasons are numerous as to why 108 -- no one knows for sure.

They range in explanation from the idea that 108 is a Harshad number (Harshad in Sanskrit, means *"great joy")* to it is an integer divisible by the sum of its digits; to there are 108 forms of dance in the Indian traditions.

I am not suggesting that you teach your child to recite Sanskrit mantras, nor any mantra 108 times. However, she can create her own personal mantra to boost her confidence or self-esteem to address an issue on which she is working. A benefit of mantras is that it gives one a focal point. For a child, it can be another form of an affirmation offering a way to positive self-talk. According to David J. Abbott, known as the "Positive Thinking Doctor," the law of positive self-talk states, "You can change who you are by changing what you say when you talk to your mind." This concept is quite empowering to teach a child. For example, if a child is nervous about taking a spelling test, she can create a personal mantra to boost her confidence by repeating, "I know my words and I am good at spelling." Suggest she recite the mantra quietly to herself while she is walking to school or riding the bus.

Another idea is to create a family mantra you can recite while doing a chore or an activity together. It can be an issue or philosophy you might like to instill. For example, maybe you are having an issue with sharing between siblings and you want to teach the karmic principle of what you give comes back to you. You can suggest to your children that they recite or sing several times; *"When I share, others will share with me."* This should be done as a fun activity, not a punishment. It should feel playful. Maybe you even start out with making up a silly mantra when something funny happens. You can play around with these by singing your mantra to different tunes or asking each child to sing the same mantra in a funny voice. As always, make the process fun and it will be remembered.

The Effect of Thoughts and Emotions on Water

A Japanese scientist named Dr. Masaru Emoto has been experimenting with the effect that words and thoughts have on water. He wrote, "One way to look at words is to consider them the switch for turning on or off the vibration of everything in the universe." In his numerous experiments, he has demonstrated how water reacts to the influences it is exposed to by forming different types of crystals when it is frozen.

Because a picture is worth a thousand words, I highly recommend getting one of Dr. Emoto's books from the library or go to his website at www.masaru-emoto.com. The pictures and videos are amazing and will be quite explicit even to a young child. You will see through the pictures that the water, under scientific conditions, responds to the thoughts placed onto it by changing its crystal make up. Good thoughts show pictures of beautiful water crystals while bad thoughts show ugly photos. Clear streams show magical crystals while polluted water shows deformed, hideous ones. According to Emoto, "Water is a mirror of our mind." He goes on to say that,"A wondrous power resides within the human soul. We hear all the time that our actions are a result of our thoughts, and this principle is truly demonstrated in how water forms crystals according to what influences it has been exposed to."

"Water is the principle of all things," wrote Thales, the Greek philosopher in 2500 BC. In appreciation of this fact that water is a vital component of life here on Earth, Dr. Emoto wrote, "The thoughts in our hearts have an impact on all life and creation of our world tomorrow." He describes an experiment on two plants. On one he wrote, "thank you" on the seed packet, flowerpot and watering can. On the other he wrote, "you fool" on each of the same things. Every day he thanked one plant and called the other a fool. The plant that he thanked grew large and lush while the one called " a fool" grew a deformed stem and wrinkled leaves.

The recognition and appreciation of these studies is especially important when one considers that the earth is made up of 70 percent water and so are we! Explain to your children that their bodies are made up of mostly water. Talk about how the water they drink will absorb their thoughts as it flows throughout their entire body. That is why we want to have healthy, positive thoughts and why sometimes when we think a scary or bad thought we can make ourselves feel sick. A fun way to bring this awareness to your children is to urge them to think positive, happy thoughts and create their own labels for water bottles.

Water Bottle Labels

After visiting Dr. Emoto's website and familiarizing your child with the concept of the power of words and thoughts on water, you can make your own special water potions. Tell your child that she can think of what type of magic water she wants to make. You can also make these as gifts for friends. For example, if you know of an ailing elder, create a water bottle that says, "Good Health" on it and give it as a gift. Or if your child is going to take an important test at school and is feeling nervous about it, write the word "Confident" on the water bottle you place in her lunch box.

Labels on Water Bottles

What you will need:

- Small plastic water bottles or a metal water bottle
- Self-adhesive labels
- Markers

Take the brand labels off of the water bottles. You might prefer to purchase a reusable metal water bottle. If so, make sure it is a solid color. If it is a metal bottle, you can attach a strip of self adhesive Velcro to one side and actually make a variety of labels you can laminate to take on and off to offer a variety of messages. Have your child think up a word that she would like to instill within herself. Some suggestions might be: *love, super smart, joy, fast, gratitude, strong, and laughter.* Have her write the word, or if she is too young you can write the word on the label for her and let her decorate it. Place the label onto the bottle and drink it up when ready.

You can carry this activity further by allowing your child to choose a word to write on the family's milk or juice containers since they, too, contain water. If you have more than one child, let each choose a word for each liquid vessel. Each can take turns and keep a list of all the different thoughts each put into what was consumed each day.

You can also create bottles for special events or special occasions. For example, on a sports water bottle, you might write the words *strong, fast* or *confident.* On a bottle taken to school for lunch you might write *smart, focused* or *inspired.* If writing directly onto the plastic, a permanent marker will work best. If you have a water machine or a water filter pitcher, write on those as well. I write on the side of all of my Poland Springs water bottles. I was hoping to make an impact on the world, one water bottle at a time, but Poland Springs wouldn't take them back with my "scribble" on them. Therefore, I learned that a little nail polish remover takes off the writing quite easily.

You can also place a message on the side of your water heater for love, or health that will impact all the water that passes through it into your home.

Spreading the Awareness

You can download the photos from Dr. Emoto's website and make gifts for family, friends and teachers. Here are some gift ideas:

Coasters

What you will need:

- **Photos from the website**
- **Construction paper or card stock**
- **Scissors**
- **Laminate**
- **Markers, crayons or pens**

Decide how big you want your coasters. A typical one is usually around 3 inches x 3 inches. If you choose, you can get creative and cut out different shapes from the card stock or paper such as a triangle, circle or diamond. Cut out and glue the photos to fit onto the paper size you chose. If you want, you can write what the picture describes on the back or include a personal message. Once the glue is dry, laminate each coaster between clear contact paper or bring them to a copy center for professional lamination. Choose a few different pictures to make up a set. Wrap up the set in a ribbon and give them to your friends and family for a unique, thought provoking gift.

Cards

What you will need:

- **Photos from the website**
- **Blank note cards or folded over construction paper**
- **Envelopes**
- **Markers**
- **Clear cellophane**

You can purchase blank note card sets at a craft store. Download the photos and glue them onto the front of the blank cards. Have your child decorate the inside or write a verse to explain the photo on the front. You can write the address for Dr. Emoto's website on the very back of the card so others to whom you send the cards can learn more about the effect of thoughts on water. This way you can send a personal message and spread awareness at the same time.

The Importance of Water Conservation

When talking about water, don't forget to include how it is a valuable resource and how we must appreciate and conserve water whenever we can. You can play a game that will reinforce this idea. Begin by asking, "How many ways do you use water everyday?" You can begin with an example for yourself such as,

"I use water to wash our clothes and dishes." Let your children give an example that is relevant to them. For example, Joey, who is a hockey player, uses water when he skates. Maisie, who takes a pottery class, uses it to help shape her clay.

Don't forget to also discuss ideas of how they might be able to conserve or save water such as turning off the water while they brush their teeth and then turning it back on when they are ready to rinse. You might want to come up with a family list of how to save water in your home. Hang it in a place where everyone can see and reach it so they can add to it if they think of something new.

CHAPTER 20

THE MIND / BODY CONNECTION

"I admit thoughts influence the body."
ALBERT EINSTEIN

As scientists discover new processes more information is avail-able on the interconnectedness between the mind, personal experience and the health of the body. This cause and effect relationship begins at birth. Sensory stimulation is necessary in order to effect positive physical growth and development. This is evident from observing children living in Eastern European orphanages. They receive shelter and nutrition, but minimal af-fection, touch or love. The results show that these children's growth has been stymied by 30 percent or more compared to children of comparable age who do receive love and touch. From this information, some are now concluding that love is the essential nutrient required for not only psychological develop-ment but healthy physical development as well.

For centuries the mind-body connection has been respect-ed and accepted in Eastern medicine practices. Now, many in the Western medicine mentality are beginning to acknowledge the interplay between our thought patterns and their effect on our bodies and our health. In a simple way, I think of how the power of a mother's kiss can heal almost every boo-boo experienced by a toddler. In that simple act of love, the pain is swept away and forgotten by the child.

If you believe our thoughts create our experiences and choices, then it is empowering to think you have played a vital impact on creating your body and the type of health you experience. Deepak Chopra, a medical doctor and renowned author, now teaches about the mind/body connection. He claims that "Every cell is made up of two ingredients: awareness and energy." Others in this field claim it is when this energy becomes blocked that *dis-ease*, *dis-order* and *dis-harmony* occurs in the body.

Louise Hay, author of *Heal your Body,* claims that all disease is a matter of negative mental patterns. She has spent years deciphering how different thoughts effect various parts of the body. She claims that by releasing the underlying negative thought patterns, the disease can often be cured. This may account for why some "miracles" occur when people are able to heal themselves from bleak medical diagnosis through visualization, intent and affirmations.

Most of us have experienced physical symptoms we know originated from an emotional source. When I was a competitive gymnast, I would experience the typical butterflies in my stomach, along with the surge of energy from the adrenaline rush prior to mounting up onto the balance beam during a competition. Learning how to control these physical symptoms through mental training and discipline was one of the ways I was able to be consistent in my performances. While others, unable to control their emotions, allowed their nerves to get the better of them.

The most profound mind-body connection I experienced occurred for me the morning my youngest son, Jake, was heading off to college. I had experienced my older son going to an out-of-state college, so consciously I wasn't feeling the trauma of him leaving "the nest" like so many first time parents do. In my rational mind I was excited for him and planned to fly out to Virginia, with him and his dad, to get him settled into this new stage of his life.

The morning he was to leave I awoke with severe abdominal pains. The pains were so severe I couldn't sit up. I frantically called my husband who had already left for work and asked him to return. Knowing I would never do that unless I was in serious trouble he promptly returned to find me doubled over in pain. As the time grew closer for us to leave, I had to tell Jake, through tears, that I couldn't go. There was just no way I could get from Boston to Virginia when I couldn't even sit up in bed or take a sip of water without experiencing excruciating pain. Throughout the morning I wreathed in pain until my sister picked me up to go to see my doctor.

The doctor sent me to the emergency room thinking I was having a gallbladder attack. After several tests with no abnormalities, the hospital physician thought perhaps it was an ulcer and sent me home with a medication to reduce stomach acid. This was difficult for me to understand because I had never experienced any stomach issues in my entire life. I also practice a holistic approach to my health so the thought of ingesting a medication everyday didn't sit very well with me.

However, for the next three days I took the medication along with a few sips of water. I could barely swallow without developing severe stomach pains, and I still could not consume any food. Because the doctor planted the seed into my head that I might have a medical condition, I began to believe it might be so, even though I had no previous history to suggest this possibility. I tried to use the power of my mind to rationalize my bodily symptoms, but none of it made sense to me, and I wasn't buying it.

On the fourth day I was able to begin to eat and felt fine. I began to research different changes I might have to make in my diet to prevent this type of painful experience from happening again believing I might have an ulcer. However, by the fifth day I said to myself, "I am not a sick person and I have nothing wrong with me." I stopped taking the medication, ate what I wanted and have never had a stomach issue since.

In hindsight, I think back to the words I chose to describe my pain to the several doctors I saw during this medical episode. I described my pain as "like childbirth in my gut." My illness was diagnosed by my own words. Jake is my baby and we are extremely close. His leaving home for a school in Virginia was severing the figurative umbilical cord that we as parents hold onto, all those years our children are under our careful watch and guidance.

What was amazing to me was how real the pain was. Whether there was a physical or emotional cause for the pain, the experience of the pain was real. It showed me how we are so connected to our children on a variety of levels for which we may not even be consciously aware.

Fortunately, Jake did fine moving in without me just as most of our children usually do. As parents, we think our children need our hand-holding every step of the way. In reality, if we prepare them to believe in their own abilities by offering them the opportunities to rely on themselves when they are young, they will be prepared for the new challenges they meet along their path.

The biologist Dr. Bruce Lipton, a former medical school professor and research scientist and, author of *The Biology of Belief,* takes the mind-body notion a step further. Dr. Lipton produced scientific findings going against the long-held dogma that genes controlled life. He wrote, "This new awareness reveals that our genes are constantly being remodeled in response to life experiences."

This scientific information is critical for the belief that we are not born victims to our family genes. Especially "bad" genes that we used to believe might predispose us to diseases like cancer or Alzheimer's. Instead, this awareness empowers us to rewrite our genes by changing our perceptions and beliefs. This research provides even more support for the powers of the mind and its persuasiveness over our bodies.

I could cite many research findings proving there is a connection between our thoughts and our health, but what does it mean for you as a parent? Firstly, if our cells are responsive to our environment, then as parents, we are responsible for the environment our children perceive themselves to live in. We obviously assume this responsibility by making a great effort to create a safe environment within which our children can thrive. We take even greater measures to provide healthy, nutritious foods to nourish their bodies. But the greatest amount of effort we need to take is to provide an atmosphere of trust, harmony and love to support our child's emotional and physical growth. Researchers have shown that the brain is influenced by emotions requiring a positive, loving environment for proper brain development and overall growth.

From this premise, an environment built out of love, positive encouragement and open mindedness to a variety of beliefs will create not only emotionally healthy children but will promote children who are physically stronger and more resilient to disease. According to Deepak Chopra, "Our body is the metabolic end product of our sensory experiences and our interpretation of these sensory experiences."

Being aware of this connection may offer you a unique insight into your child's total wellbeing. Think of the old stereotype of the child who fakes a stomachache because she doesn't want to go to school. According to Louise Hay, a stomach problem is caused by "dread and fear of the new" both symptoms which could be a common experience for a child attending school. She also claims that headaches, quite typical for teenage girls, are representative of self-criticism and fear. Both are feelings many teenage girls would acknowledge. It is important that when your child displays physical symptoms, you tune in to her underlying emotions. If you begin a pattern of talking about feelings as freely as you discuss physical symptoms, then your child will feel comfortable coming to you with all of her complaints.

Tuning into our bodies and how they speak to us through our symptoms takes practice. It also takes a parent who is sensitive and aware enough to her child's needs to truly listen and not be quick to dismiss what is ailing the child. If your child is constantly complaining of a physical symptom prior to a specific activity, then perhaps there is an emotional component to her disorder. Maybe the activity is causing her emotional stress, which is causing her physical disease.

For a young child, the cause and effect pattern between an ailment and a stress factor like a stomachache prior to an upcoming test may appear relatively obvious. But for abstract issues like the middle schooler being bullied, or the teen who has low self-esteem around her body, exploring your child's feelings with her may prevent physical manifestations like depression or anorexia.

Emotion is "energy in motion." According to ancient Chinese medicine and mind-body practitioners, it is when this energy becomes blocked that disease sets in. Open communication and sensitive listening on your part will allow your child to express her emotions without fear of judgment, allowing the negative energy, such as stress, to pass freely out of her system.

One way for everyone, including children, to connect to their thoughts and bodies, is by practicing meditation and stillness. You are probably rolling your eyes right now saying, "Yah, right! Meditation is hard enough for adults to do, how is my nonstop, eight-year-old dynamo going to be able to do it?" In the following chapter are some fun suggestions of how to slow things down in our hectic lives. Meditation doesn't have to be hours long. You can introduce a simple practice of mindfulness and breathing that requires just a few minutes each day.

CHAPTER 21

BEING IN THE MOMENT: PRACTICING STILLNESS

"Your innermost sense of self, of who you are, is inseparable from stillness. This is the I Am that is deeper than name and form."
ECKHART TOLLE

Living in the moment and being present in your body, with no negative thoughts to distract you, are ideas you may only attach to your yoga class that you squeezed in between dropping the children off to school, answering your emails and shopping for groceries. For so many of us, our mindset is that we always have to be doing something or else we are wasting time. This frenetic pace of life flows to our children whom we constantly feel the need to entertain. From the time they wake up, our children are externally stimulated by TV, computers, electronic devices and scheduled activities. Rarely are our children left to entertain themselves for extended periods of time. David Elkind wrote in his book *Power Of Play,* "Parents, anxious for their children to succeed in an increasingly global economy, regard play as a luxury that the contemporary child cannot afford." Our children are so programmed by structured activities and electronics that they no longer know how to entertain themselves through imagination and play. Even car rides, which used to be an opportunity for conversation, have become silent because everyone is entertained by their personal electronics or individual DVD player.

Living in the Moment

Children are born knowing how to be present in the moment. Have you ever seen two children happily playing until one child grabs the other's toy? Then you'll see a full-blown melt down, complete with tears and screams of protest. When the toy is regained, the tears and anger are quickly forgotten with the toy thief once again welcome to play along. There are no grudges or resentment to hold onto, carrying forward into the future.

Being able to be with yourself without distractions is essential in order for children to discover what intrigues them about the world. It allows them to be guided by their instinct because the sound of what is driving them is not drowned out by over-stimulation. Children need silence and stillness to discover what is in their heart. Infants are born with this capacity.

Everyday, infants are toted along with their older sibling into my classroom and plunked down on the floor. There they remain silently entertaining themselves, staring up at the ceiling fan, sucking on their fingers or playing with their toes. Usually, they are only heard from when the natural forces of hunger or gas disrupt their peaceful bliss. They are just as content with observing their surroundings as they are by fancy rattles or toys that are presented to them. This is demonstrated by the fact that they often throw the toy to the floor.

I have observed babies left in these buckets for an entire one-and-a-half hour class. Often they are turned towards the wall and they still are content to just be. What is this telling us? Maybe it suggests that the need for stimulation is accumulative. The more we offer and pull our children out of this innate state of contentment the more we have to feed the frenzy. The need to be busy becomes addictive, resulting in our children needing constant stimulation. When they don't have it, they complain they are bored, and drive us crazy so we end up signing them up for more activities leading to overstimulation for them and stress for us.

Child development expert, David Elkind, best known for his book *The Hurried Child* wrote, "During the past two decades children have lost 12 hours of free time a week, including eight hours of unstructured play and outdoor activities. In contrast, the amount of time children spend in organized sports has doubled, while the number of minutes children devote to passive spectator leisure has increased five fold." Time to relax and just be present in the moment has become obsolete in the hurried world into which we have thrust our children. I know many mothers who have expressed that their second or third child rarely sleeps in her crib for nap times since they are constantly on the move being toted along to the activities of their older siblings.

Without the opportunity to train ourselves as children to fill our free time, we become adults who get nervous and feel guilty about time that is not filled. My husband actually said to me, "I'm bad" to describe how he feels about himself for sleeping an extra hour on a Sunday morning! This self-induced pressure for every minute to be productive and accounted for is like a treadmill that won't turn off. Eventually we end up exhausted, depleted and questioning if this is what life is all about. Usually, it is only when our body breaks down that we begin to have the awareness that life isn't always meant to live in high gear. We then begin to search for ways to teach ourselves how to unlearn the pace to which we have become addicted.

We drag our children to play groups, music, art and gym classes several times a week before they are even two years old. In my program, I allow children the opportunity to make up a missed class. Unfortunately, many mothers are unable to take advantage of this benefit because the child already has something scheduled for every day. Sometimes, children attend two classes in one day and they are only one year old.

Alvin Rosenfeld, author of the book *The Over- scheduled Child,* coined the term "hyper-parenting" for this type of behavior. He wrote, "The term 'hyper-parent' means that by controlling all our children's activities, they will become successful. Actually, it's more than a term, it's a way of life." Unfortunately, this pace is not only unhealthy for the child but causes stress for mothers too. Some of this overstimulation frenzy comes from the misnomer that parents are responsible for the development of our children's brains. This idea has placed enormous responsibility onto parents who feel they are directly depriving their child of intellect later in life if they do not tap into critical periods of learning by providing educational toys and an abundance of stimulating opportunities during the early years. It comes from the heart's desire for wanting the most for our children, but quickly becomes an obsession based on external pressures. In her book *Perfect Madness* Judith Warner wrote, "The more women bought into the crazy competitiveness of our time, the more they tended to suffer as mothers."

This belief that we have the power to affect our children's brain growth was initiated from research performed on rats back in the 1960s and 1970s. It concluded that rats living in enriched environments developed larger brains than those being raised in isolation. People then made the assumption, (and we know never to make assumptions), that this would hold true for children too. However, it is extremely rare for a child to be raised in isolation and deprived of any stimulation. The natural environment offers hearing language, exploring tastes and seeing new sights that constantly stimulate children.

In the book *Einstein Never Used Flashcards*, the authors cite Professor Mark Rosenzweig of Berkeley University, who observed, "The rats that remained in nature had the best brains of all. They were stimulated by the sights, sounds, and smells of the world around them...In other words, their natural environment was the best thing in the world for their rat brains - even better than the Disneyland the researchers created in their cages." Of course, toy manufacturers did not promote this aspect of his findings. Instead they capitalized on the aspect that would support building an entire empire of educational products built on false promises to make your child smarter.

If you have been taken in by the myth that expensive educational toys, videos, or computer programs will make your child smarter, then now is the time to take a sigh of relief. There is no need to feel guilty if you cannot afford the latest promise to advance your child's cognitive abilities. There is no concrete evidence to prove the connection between particular educational programs or techniques and brain development. You may think you are motivating your child to become an aspiring musician or mathematician by listening to Mozart. But in reality, she is learning just as much from pounding on the pots and pans. What has been found to be true is that learning occurs best in context. What children need are not things, but you. As James Russell Lowell wrote, "The best academy - a mother's knee."

In the book *Einstein Never Used Flashcards*, the authors suggest that parents take a new approach towards research and media hype. They suggest that instead of reacting in haste to the parenting fad of the times, implement the three R's: *reflect, resist*, and *re-center.* Experts agree on one thing and that is, young children need lots of time, attention and love from significant others in their lives. For example, it has been shown that the best way to learn language and build a strong vocabulary isn't through an interactive computer game, but through open-ended conversation with adults.

Overscheduling of structured activities is also the result of this competitive philosophy of needing to excel at something. I have a two-year-old in my class who loves to sing and dance to all the music in class. When I was affirming his love of music with his mother, the first thing she said to me was," I was thinking of signing him up for a singing class since he sings all day at home." My first inclination was to ask, why? He is already doing what he loves on his own, motivated by his internal passion. Certainly a two-year-old isn't asking to take singing lessons.

A similar philosophy holds true for school-age children. If a child shows an interest or a natural talent for a sport, they are automatically placed on a competitive team or enrolled in structured classes to train their talent. Young children are over coached and pushed to train their God-given talents, often creating physical and emotional stress. What parents need to understand is that if this talent is truly your child's calling, then nothing will stop her from developing it. Artistic children will draw, naturally athletic children will move and musical children will tap out a song with anything they can find.

Before enrolling for one more activity that you will have to pay for and drive to, ask yourself, "Is this because they need it?" Or, is the real truth, that you need and want it? Being a mother of young children can be quite tedious. Classes appear to be a win/win because they offer children a stimulating opportunity and mothers the social situations we crave. The need to search out social opportunities through classes is partly a new need created by living in the suburbs where motherhood often comes with a sense of isolation, loneliness and boredom. However, using your child to solve your social needs through scheduled activities can be exhausting for your child and expensive for you. Ultimately this creates more stress for everyone. It is no wonder that many mothers end up feeling more like a chauffeur than a parent for a majority of their parenting years.

Instead, if you are a mother of preschool children, try to organize time with other mothers who have a similar philosophy concerning the need for open-ended play. Each week, pick a setting to meet that offers unstructured play opportunities. For example, plan to meet every Tuesday at 9:30 at a playground, a park, a zoo or a museum. Divide up the weeks so that each mother takes one week to plan the event. This will offer diversity and spread out the responsibility. Before leaving each week, make sure you know who is responsible for the next week's event.

If you have school-age children, you can organize a non-competitive soccer game, a hike in the woods or enjoy hanging out at home with no agenda. This will create opportunities for open-ended play such as drawing with sidewalk chalk, riding bikes, or doing arts and crafts.

The American Academy of Pediatrics says that overscheduling for children can lead to increased stress, anxiety and physical ailments. Offering your child opportunities to practice stillness is a gift she will carry with her throughout her life. It will also offer you some benefits as well. One thing you can do together is to practice being still through fun activities. Teaching your child how to be still and silent for brief periods of time will have benefits for the both of you. This can be the beginning of a meditation practice. If you are thinking that this will be impossible, try cuddling your child on your lap. Have you ever noticed just how long a child will be still and quiet when embraced, hugged or touched?

Stillness Games

You can practice stillness with your children in fun, creative ways. You may be saying to yourself, "It's hard enough to get my active six-year-old to sit still long enough to eat!" However, stillness can actually be fun to practice. Stillness of your body requires body awareness, concentration and discipline. Children are capable even if only for a few seconds. Believing they are capable is the first step in encouraging them to play. The idea is not to say, "Now we are going to practice being still so we can learn to be more peaceful." The idea is to make a game out of the practice without your child knowing they're practicing.

Stop and Go with Music

My one-to-two-year-olds are quite capable of doing this game. You probably played a form of it yourself as a child but not with the intention of practicing stillness. It is a game that also teaches listening skills, body awareness and body control. To begin, turn on some music and tell your child that when the music stops they are going to be still and quiet. You can add an instrument to make this more fun. In my class, we use wrist bells. You can use a pot and cooking spoon or any other music making instrument you might have around the house.

For older children, you can incorporate their whole body by playing "freeze dancing." You can pick different types of songs that will encourage different types of dancing styles such as rock and roll, salsa or classical. Tell them to dance to the music until you turn it off. When the music is silent, the idea is to freeze in a certain pose. You can extend the length of time the music is off as the children get better and better at being still.

"Boss" Your Body

I also like to use the term "boss" your body for young children. It is important for children to understand that they are in control of their own bodies. Here is a fun game you can do anywhere. Have your child sit on the floor with knees bent in front of her. Have her run in place really fast until you say, "stop." Bring the awareness of her ability to control her body by saying, "You can really "boss" your feet. This is important because when I say 'stop,' if you are running towards the street, you are going to know how. That is so awesome!"

Allow your child to choose a part of the body to move and then allow her to dictate to you when to stop moving. For example, she might pick flapping her arms like a bird or hopping on one leg. This will offer her the experience of being in control and demonstrate that she can control all of her body parts equally. Body awareness is important when she knows she can control her hands if an older sibling grabs something away from her. You can end the game by being silly saying, "I can't control my hands" and then begin to tickle her.

Simple Yoga Poses

As your child masters the idea of stop and go games, introduce some simple yoga exercises. Yoga for children offers intriguing names such as "tree pose," "three-legged dog," "inchworm" and "warrior one." The tree pose is done by standing on one leg. Place the free foot alongside the middle of your inner thigh with your knee turned out to the side. Hands can begin at the center of the chest pressed together in prayer fashion. Once your child is stable, have her raise her hands overhead. Explain to her that her arms are like the tree when it grows upwards towards the sky. She will try this simple yoga pose because of the name. It is something she is familiar with and allows her to use her imagination. Ask her to count how long she can balance by counting her breaths. It is helpful for her to have a visual marker. Tell her to try to gently stare at one thing and that will help her to balance and keep still. Make sure she tries this on each leg and ask her if one side was easier than the other. This is often the case.

Try not to make this a competition between children but more of a challenge for each child to try to hold the pose as long as they want. If they wobble, tell them that is exactly what a tree does. A tree is meant to be flexible with the wind so it can move from side to side. You can even pretend to try and blow them over by blowing on them.

A downward dog pose is another favorite for children because of the name. Have your child place both hands and feet on the floor. The feet are hips' distance apart and the hands are placed shoulder-distance apart. The hands are placed out in front enough to give an angle or slight pike to the body. If you demonstrate your child most likely will be able to copy you in a couple of tries.

The three-legged dog pose is similar to downward dog but one leg is lifted in the air. Once again, the hands are used on the floor for balance and support.

The warrior one pose is similar to a lunge but the back foot is flat and turned at a 45-degree angle. Arms are stretched straight overhead by the ears. These are just a few yoga poses that require balance and stillness. There are many others that you can learn by taking a class yourself or watching a DVD. Most cable stations offer yoga classes that will give you a good visual of the poses.

At the end of most yoga classes one practices *savasana.* Teachers will often describe savasana as the most important part of the yoga practice. It offers practicing stillness and relaxation by having you lay completely flat, arms by your side, utilizing slow and relaxed breath. This is called the corpse pose.

You can have your child practice savasana by calling it a different name. I call it the Mummy Game. Tell her she is going to be like a mummy frozen in time, laying very still until you unfreeze her. Make sure she is comfortable. You can place a small pillow under her knees and a light blanket on top of her if she desires. If she seems to fidget, you can have her hold something in each hand. I suggest a smooth crystal like aquamarine or aventurine. These stones will help her to relax. You can call them her relaxing magic jewels. After all, mummies often were buried with jewels. I will talk more about crystals and their healing powers in sections to come.

While she is in this pose you can play quiet music, tell a short story, offer a guided meditation or take her through a body awareness exercise. If you are using music, pick out a piece that is not too long to start, maybe only two minutes in length, and increase the time as she gets more comfortable with the game. I suggest you try music instead of telling her a story since this will offer you the opportunity to relax and experience the benefits of being still, too. I can guarantee that two minutes of being still while doing nothing will give you more of a recharge than a Venti espresso at Starbucks.

Being still together will offer your child a role model. It will also offer you awareness of what it is like to step out of the busyness of life for a few moments, which is what you want your child to experience. It also demonstrates to your child that she has your undivided attention. This is often a rare commodity in hectic schedules.

If you choose to tell her a short story or guided meditation, make sure it is one that will challenge her imagination but offer a relaxing experience. For example, you might say, "Imagine you are lying on a soft blanket in the middle of a field. The grass feels soft and warm against your back. The sun is out and it begins to warm up your toes. Now your legs are starting to feel tingly and warm, too. Next, your tummy feels warm and full, like you just finished eating your favorite meal. Now the sun is moving over your chest, warming your heart and smiling at you. Now it is warming your arms and fingers until your whole body is perfectly warm and content in the light of the sun. The sky is a bright blue and you are watching the clouds float by above you. First there is a cloud that floats by in the shape of an elephant. You watch it pass overhead until it melts back into the blue sky. Next, there is one in the shape of a bird that flies right overhead. Oh look, now I see one coming in the shape of a large heart. I think it wants me to tell you that I love you." This is just an example of a guided meditation that also allows her to practice awareness of individual body parts.

Meditation for Children

Savasana is the beginning of a meditation practice. Meditation does require practice. Although the physiological and mental benefits have been scientifically proven, most of us can hardly find the time or patience to commit to a consistent meditation practice. Just because we have a difficult time with it as adults, doesn't mean that children won't be open to it. Unlike adults, whose thoughts tend to be logical with a sense of purpose, children are naturally captivated by their own imaginative thoughts.

There are many benefits that meditation offers children. Besides offering them the opportunity to relax, meditation teaches them to be more attentive. It offers them the opportunity to explore their imagination without limitation. It also offers them the opportunity to practice a behavior or work through feelings in their heads prior to having to act them out in the real world. For example, Sarah practices how to feel and let go of her fear of dogs through a meditation so when she interacts with one in real life she is able to cope better with her feelings of anxiety.

To begin, explain to your child that meditation is a big word that can be done in a variety of ways. Tell her it means closing her eyes, breathing calmly and letting her mind wonder to a place she wants it to go. To demonstrate how her mind can take her places, you can have her sit comfortably and close her eyes. Ask her to describe her bedroom to you. After she is finished, explain to her that even though she isn't in her bedroom, her mind can take her there. That is a little what meditation is like. It can take you to any place you want to be.

The next step is that it's important to be comfortable. She can pick whether she wants to be sitting or lying down. I suggest that you initially find a special place in your home that will offer both of you the opportunity to be comfortable and experience quiet without interruption for an extended period of time. You wouldn't want to set up in the family room if big brother is due home with his friends to play Xbox after school.

As she becomes more comfortable with the practice, make sure you explain that she can meditate anywhere. Let her know that if she is feeling stressed or anxious, she can simply close her eyes and take a few deep breaths to help calm herself. She can do this at school, before a soccer game, or waiting in a line. This will give her a great sense of control against the stresses that continually bombard children from the harshness of the "real world."

There are several books about teaching children how to meditate as well as numerous articles online. Kerry Lee Maclean has written two adorable books for the younger child about meditation. One is called *Moody Cow Meditates* and the other is *Peaceful Piggy Meditation.* Another book for slightly older children is one by Gail Silver called *Anh's Anger.*

Most importantly, if you are going to move from playing the stillness games into a meditation practice, then I encourage you to be consistent and find the time to practice on a regular basis. Just as one needs repetition to become good at any skill, so it is with meditation. If you don't participate in a regular meditation practice, then let your child be your guide. If she is enjoying it, or asks to do it with you and appears to be benefiting from it, then I would encourage you to set aside time on a regular basis to do it with her. Who knows, through the process, she may lead you to a place you need to go.

CHAPTER 22

Numbers, Numerology and Math

"Mathematics is the language with which
God has written the universe."
GALILEO GALILEI

Galileo's quote describes the fact that numerical patterns, ratios and sequences are amazingly present in nature, the universe and even our own human bodies. Some of you may be aware of the term the *golden ratio*. The golden ratio is an irrational mathematical constant, approximately 1.61803398874989 often denoted by the Greek letter Phi. The golden ratio has puzzled the best minds since its discovery. It has been discovered to be contained in great architectural achievements like the pyramids, paintings by artistic masters like Leonardo da Vinci and Salvador Dali and musical compositions by Chopin. The golden ratio has inspired historians, architects, artists and mystics like no other number in the history of mathematics.

The golden ratio is found throughout nature. One example is in the number of spirals found in the center of sunflowers. It is also profoundly visible in the proportions of the human body. The golden ratio is the exact measurement between the distance of specific body parts such as the distance between our fingers and elbow, our navel to the top of our head and between our pupils, just to name a few. It is also present in the structure of the lungs and has even been connected to the helixes of our DNA. Once again, we see that nothing in life is random. Everything is precisely as it should be by divine design.

Numbers are an inherent part of our existence. Deepak Chopra wrote, "Mathematics expresses values that reflect the cosmos, including orderliness, balance, harmony, logic, and abstract beauty." Numbers even played an important role in your first connection to your child. The idea that you might be pregnant originated in the concept of the number of days your period was late. Then came the baby's due date and the counting of how many weeks pregnant you were. Not to mention how much weight you gained. At birth, your baby was assigned a birth date, a time of birth, a birth weight, a length, as well as her first numerical score on the Apgar test. Before she had even left the delivery room, she had already acquired many numbers to describe and assess her. Numbers play a significant role in our lives in a variety of ways. It is therefore worth exploring the idea that has been around for thousands of years in the science of numerology.

Numerology

The metaphysical science of numerology dates back thousands of years. Egypt and Babylon are cited as the earliest cultures to use numerology. It is based in the belief that every number has a distinct energy or vibrational pattern which impacts on your life. Each letter of the alphabet has been assigned a given number, so your birth name, as well as your birth date, have an important energetic influence over your life.

Although he didn't create it, Pythagoras, a Greek mathematician and mystic living around 590 BC, has been assigned the title of the father of numerology. Pythagoras studied the theory behind numbers and believed there was a universal order to everything. He said that everything was related to mathematics and numbers were the ultimate reality. He also believed that objects contained a vibrational energy with positive energy exhibiting greater force than negative energy. Pythagoras taught his *Science of Numbers and Theory of Magnitude* in a school of learning in Crotona, a Greek colony in southern Italy. Once again, like many ancient teachings, his were to be kept secret. Therefore, his students were not allowed to write down any information. His students adhered to this rule until his death and his teachings were almost lost to the modern world. Dr. Juno Jordan wrote, "Pythagoras taught his students an exact mathematical precision. The principles governing the numbers were understood to be the principles of real existence; the elements of numbers were the elements of realities."

In the 1900s, Dr. Julia Seton is credited with naming the science of the study of numbers as "numerology." Her granddaughter, Dr. Juno Jordan, known for her book, *The Romance in Your Name,* and founder of the California Institute of Numerical research, is also considered to be a major influential force behind what numerology has grown to become today.

To begin to understand numerology, you must first learn that every letter of the alphabet has a correlated numerical influence assigned to it. Each individual has five core numbers that, according to numerology, greatly influence your life. (Please note that individual books may call the same number by a different name.) The first is your *birthday.* Your *Life Path* number is determined from your full birth date (month, day and year.) Your *Expression* number is derived from the letters of your birth name as it appears on your birth certificate. Your *Hearts Desire* is determined from the vowels of your birth name. Your *Personality* number comes from the consonants of your birth name. There are also several other numerical influences that create a numerology chart. All interact with these core numbers.

If you would like to learn more about numerology, I recommend *The Complete Idiot's Guide to Numerology* by Lagerquist & Lenard. It is easy to follow and it will offer you step-by-step guidance on how to figure out one's core numbers. Juno Jordan's book, *The Romance In Your Name,* is also an excellent resource. She has a small section on numerology and understanding your child's personal year. Ellin Dodge's book, *Numerology Has Your Number,* also describes how the numbers influence us in childhood. If an older child wants to explore numerology on her own, I like Tatiania Hardie's book, *Tatiania's Book of Numerology.* It is quite colorful and easy to navigate with less emphasis placed on the calculating and more emphasis placed on the influences of each number. There are also many websites that can give you an overview of numerology.

If you are intrigued by numerology, I recommend having a professional reading done by an experienced numerologist. She will be able to reveal other numerical influences such as your pinnacle dates, challenge numbers, personal year, maturity, essence and transit influences. If you seek out a professional, make sure she has had several years of experience, provides you with either a written copy or a recording of your reading so you can refer back to it.

According to numerology, your child's name, and how you chose to spell it, will greatly influence her. So before you even set out on your parenting role, you had a major influence on your child's journey by choosing her name. Lagerquist & Lenard wrote in *The Complete Idiot's Guide to Numerology,* "You're choosing for another soul the pattern for his or her lifetime on Earth." At the same time, numerologists believe that you shouldn't name a child solely based on pre-calculated numbers. In other words, you shouldn't choose a name because its' energy adds up to encourage power, creativity or wealth. Numerologists encourage parents to wait until the child is born and then let your instinct guide you to choose a name that you feel is right for that specific child. The *Complete Idiot's Guide to Numerology* claims your name reveals:

> ". your life purpose
> . what you must live up to in this lifetime
> . your opportunities for success
> . your spiritual mission
> . the qualities and manner of living you must develop
> . what you are destined for
> . the target you are aiming for in life
> . the kind of work that will be a natural expression for your life path."

What numerology will offer you is an awareness and an understanding of a invisible force that affects you, others and particularly your children. It offers information as to what years are more influenced by specifics types of energies over others. This can help determine what type of action to take or not take. For example, 2011 was a nine-year for me in my life cycle. The energy behind a nine is one of completion and closure. It is not a time to start something new. When I consulted with my numerologist about this book, she suggested that I spend the entire nine year completing the manuscript. She advised not to send it out for publication until the next year, which was a one year for me. The one energy is that of new beginnings which would benefit the book. She further explained that if one tries to start something new in a nine year, it usually will fail because the universal energy isn't supporting it.

This was great advice since I wanted the book to be a success and a pathway for me into a new career. From a psychological standpoint, this information removed a lot of pressure I was placing on myself to finish the book. Instead, I was able to take my time knowing that I had all year to complete it under the power of my nine energy. Under the influence of the one energy, I had a much better chance of success at something new in my life like getting this book to print!

Numerology can be used to gain insight about the timing of life's big events such as taking a new job, getting married, moving to a specific numbered house, as well as seeing if you and a mate are compatible with each other. As a parent, it will offer you insight into the invisible influences that impact your child.

Dr. Juno Jordan suggests that knowing your child's personal year will help guide you in ways of understanding and parenting her. In her book *The Romance in Your Name*, she wrote, "During the five personal year, a child will not respond to rules and regulations as under a four influence. Impatience with routine and regulations will be present. More freedom should be allowed, with public interests cultivated, and encouragement should be given to take part in community activities. Restlessness, impatience, and a tendency to disregard rules and regulations are the desire to find out what life is all about." This sounds more like the entire stage of adolescence than just one personal year!

As I stated earlier, awareness offers insight. This can ultimately lead us to parent our children differently than in the past. Being aware of the power of numerology will provide you with clues you previously did not have regarding why each child lives and experiences life the way he or she does. Most mothers will agree that each of their children is quite different. Numerology explains why, since each has a different name and birth date. Even twins born on the same date will be different because although they share the same birthday, with the same

"Life Path number," they have different "Expression" numbers because of their individual names.

Possessing this knowledge can help you to determine areas of talents to pursue; ways to understand, interact and inspire each of your children. The more you understand, honor and respect each child's uniqueness, the easier your job of parenting will be. Numerology can then be considered a great parenting tool.

Having Fun with The Power of Names and Numbers

Numerology Alphabet Chart

1	2	3	4	5	6	7	8	9
A	B	C	D	E	F	G	H	I
J	K	L	M	N	O	P	Q	R
S	T	U	V	W	X	Y	Z	

Numerology is a fun way to teach your child about her uniqueness in the world. Without having to do the complicated calculations numerology requires, you can begin by simply identifying the first letter of your child's first name on the above chart. This is called her *Cornerstone*. It describes one's innate approach to life and how one responds to experience. For example:

AJS – Innovative thinker, leader, independent, ambitious and headstrong
BKT – Peaceful, cooperative, highly sensitive, a good team player
CLU – Spontaneous, creative, verbal, imaginative, loves life and to socialize
DMV – Loves order, organization and rules, is serious and hard working

ENW – Curious, adventurous, restless, imaginative, needs change and excitement

FOX – Responsible, emotional, nurturing, love of family and self sacrificing

GPY – Introspective, philosophical, perceptive, keen mind, works best alone

HQZ – Leadership ability, confident, desire for material success, inspires others

IR – Selfless, humanitarian, idealistic, great understanding and tolerance

As you can see there is great diversity in the characteristics associated with each set of letters. This tiny bit of numerology provides helpful information to harmonize your parenting with your child's intrinsic nature. For example, if your child's name begins with an A, J or S you can appreciate she is going to have her own ideas about things, will want to be the boss and may try to challenge authority. Therefore, you might offer her the opportunity to contribute her opinion about simple family decisions supporting her need for independence. This is quite different from a child born with a name beginning with a D, M or V who loves to adhere to rules, respects limits and will more than likely do what she is told. The child whose name begins with a C, L or U is going to be an imaginative, social, spark of energy. You may want to provide her with paints and lots of opportunity for imaginative play, conversation and socializing. This is quite opposite of a child whose name starts with a G, P, or Y who is introspective and would prefer investigating some intriguing topic alone on the Internet over a play date.

Children find great pleasure in identifying with the uniqueness that their name offers them. Did you ever doodle your name in bubble letters on a notebook? Or write it over and over again in a variety of designs? Identifying your child's personal numbers, unique to her, will offer another means of understanding her while helping her grow her sense of identity.

My *Cornerstone* T Shirt

What you will need:

- **T shirt**
- **Permanent markers or fabric paints**
- **Cardboard or cookie sheet**

Slide the cardboard or cookie sheet inside your T shirt. This will avoid the marker from bleeding through the fabric. Have your child draw her *Cornerstone* letter onto the front of the shirt. Flip the shirt over and on the back draw the corresponding number. So if your child's name begins with a B, K or T draw the number 2 on the back of the shirt. Using the adjectives above or a numerology reference book, discuss with your child the adjectives that coincide with her *Cornerstone* letter. Ask which ones she connects to and write those onto the shirt. Allow her to finish decorating the shirt any way she chooses.

Invisible Me Word Search

What you will need:

- **Graph paper**
- **Pen or pencil**
- **Highlighter or markers**

Before beginning, write the adjectives that coincide with your child's *Cornerstone* letter onto the graph paper with each letter in its own square. Spread the words out to cover the entire sheet of paper. Fill in the remaining blank squares with random letters. Write a list of the adjectives you used and have your child try to find each one.

For older children you can make this more complicated by making a family word search. Discuss the *Cornerstone* letter and its attributes for each family member. This is a great opportunity to discover your unique qualities and talk about your differences. Fill the paper with adjectives associated with each *Cornerstone* letter. Have your child use a different color marker or highlighter to find the words associated with each letter. For example; she can find dad's attributes and highlight them in yellow while mom's are in blue and her's are in green.

Aside from numerology, numbers may be signs given to us by the spirit realm. Doreen Virtue, PhD, known for her book, *Angel Numbers*, explains that numbers that repeatedly show up in our lives have specific message meanings from our angels watching over us. She assigns a specific meaning to each number, one through 999. She also explains how to read larger number sequences and instructs that the middle number in a three-digit number is the most important. According to Virtue, "When there are three or more numbers, the center digit is of primary focus. The angels say that this number represents the 'heart' of the matter." Many of us have had the experience of seeing the same number repeatedly on a clock, then maybe the same number on a license plate or sign and then later on a cash receipt. Virtue explains that number patterns you repeatedly see have meaning for you from your angels and you should pay attention to these messages. If this experience of seeing the same numbers repeatedly happens to you, then you might be interested in looking up the meanings of those numbers that show up for you in her book.

CHAPTER 23

CRYSTALS AND THE POWER OF MAGIC STONES

The "Bones of Mother Earth"
UNKNOWN

The beauty and allure of crystals will naturally entice children to explore them. The word crystal comes from the Greek word *krustallos,* which is derived from Krysos, meaning, ice cold. It was once thought that crystals were a type of ice that was so cold that it would never melt. Today, it is understood that crystals are composed of silicon and oxygen, which is found in the earth's core. When these two elements combine, they form quartz. There are other types of crystals and gemstones that are not quartz, such as diamonds, which are made from carbon and amber, which is made from resin. For our discussion purposes, I'll use the word crystals or stones to refer to crystals, minerals, and gemstones.

The use of crystals for healing on physical, emotional and spiritual levels, as well as for protection, rituals, luck and meditation dates back thousands of years. There are many references to crystals within the Bible. They were often used on the breastplates of the high priests of Israel. Each breastplate contained four rows of precious stones to equal 12 stones, each one representing the 12 tribes of Israel. The stones were worn for protection and wisdom.

It is theorized that the people of the legendary city of Atlantis were able to synthesize crystal energy and use it in amazing technological ways that we currently have not been able to duplicate. Crystals were used in the ancient societies of Egypt and Greece. Some believe that the building of the pyramids was done using crystal energy. The Egyptians also used crystals for healing potions, make up and to adorn artifacts. Native Americans used stones as amulets. They considered many stones to be sacred and they were often used in worship to relate to spirit guides. The Aborigines of Australia, the Mayans and Incas also used crystals for healing and spiritual practices.

History shows the use of jade in ancient China has been seen since before 3000 B.C. The Chinese believe in a symbolic link between jade and their goddess Quan Yin, the goddess of mercy. All of these ancient references, once again, remind us that many of the "new age" practices are not so new at all. The belief that crystals offered numerous benefits lasted until the 17th century when the importance of logic, reason and need for scientific proof developed. Without documented proof of their powers, skepticism about their effectiveness crept in.

Exactly how crystals work is based on the principle that everything resonates at a particular vibration. When healthy, our bodies vibrate at a certain level. When we get sick, this level gets thrown off. Crystals channel energy. They help the body do what it naturally can to heal itself. They help bring us back to a healthy level of vibration with certain types of crystals resonating with specific body parts and maladies. There are many reference guides you can search to find out what type of crystal you might look for if you are suffering from a particular illness. One such book is *The Crystal Healer* by Philip Permutt.

Another is the *Crystal Bible* by Judy Hall. Crystals can help any-thing from indigestion to asthma, depression to fertility. They can be worn as jewelry, carried in pockets or purses or placed upon the body on one of your seven chakra centers.

Understanding the seven chakras is a foundation of all energy work including Reiki and crystals. Some of you may be familiar with the term if you have taken a yoga class since many yoga poses are designed to open specific chakras.

The word *chakra* comes from the Sanskrit word "cakra" and means wheel. Chakras are said to be wheel-like spinning vortices spread out along the body from above the head to just below the base of your spine. Each chakra is correlated with a specific energy, color, tone and function. It is believed that in ancient Indian medicine, when the chakras are all spinning correctly, then one is feeling healthy, in balance and energized. When one of the chakras is vibrating out of tune, then the body experiences *dis*order or *dis*ease. The seven chakras are said by some to reflect how the unified consciousness of man (the soul), manages the physical body here on Earth.

There are many reference materials to explore chakra charts. One suggested book is *The Book of Chakras* by Ambika Wauters. Here is a brief description of each chakra, the energy associated with it, along with its corresponding color and tonal note.

Red: The root chakra, is located at the base of the spine. It's associated with survival and grounding us in the physical world. Its tonal note is C.

Orange: The sacral chakra is located just below the navel. It's associated with our sexual energy, reproductive capacity, creativity, our ability to connect to others and energy. Its tonal note is D.

Yellow: The solar plexus chakra is below your heart and is associated with our set of emotions. It gives us our sense of personal power in the world. If blocked, it manifests as anger or a sense of victimization. The tonal note associated with it is E.

Green: The heart chakra is responsible for our ability to trust, love and take risks. A blockage can result in heart problems or a lack of compassion. Its tonal note is F.

Blue: The throat chakra is all about communication and speaking your personal truth. Its tonal note is G.

Indigo: The third eye, pineal gland chakra is located between the eyebrows and is thought to be a physical eye at the base of the brain. It's responsible for our dreams, imagination, intuition and our physic abilities. Its tonal note is A.

Violet: The crown chakra is located just above the head and connects you to a higher realm through understanding, a spiritual connection and awareness. It's thought to be the chakra of consciousness. Its tonal note is B.

When using crystals as a healing tool, the crystal would be placed along the same corresponding color chakra. For example, a yellow stone would be used for any issues involving the solar plexus. A red stone would be used for the root chakra and it's corresponding energies. One nice thing about the book, *The Crystal Healer,* is that it is divided into colors of stones and by the names of physical ailments. So you can look up your physical symptom and it will give you the name of a crystal to help with that illness. Or, you can look up the color of the chakra and it will provide you with the corresponding stones and their unique healing properties.

Crystals can also help with your environment to achieve many things from increasing energy and communication to helping your plants grow. It is important to keep crystals clean and free of dust by rinsing them under water. Crystals can be recharged by placing them out in the sun or moonlight.

Even if you can't conceive that crystals have energetic or healing properties, they are fun to explore and collect with children. Sometimes, just believing that something can help, actually does. This is called the placebo effect. Did you ever have a rabbit foot or magic charm as a child that you swore gave you super powers? As a competitive gymnast, I can attest to the fact that many national competitors carried gym bags full of good luck charms to every competition. I most certainly had mine. I carried a piece of an uneven bar my coach had sawed off for me, a smooth worry stone, and a funny rubber clown I found at one of my national competitions. These were just a few I wouldn't dare to compete without.

Awareness and knowledge that crystals contain specific energetic properties will offer your child the possibility of belief. Children are all about magical thinking. Sometimes just believing in something is enough to give you the extra confidence that you might need in yourself. A sweet book that is a Caldecott winner is *Sylvester and the Magic Pebble* by William Steig. This book introduces the idea of a magic stone, as well as the idea to be careful of what you wish for because the universe is always listening.

Empowering your child by having her carry a crystal or "magic stone" will boast her confidence in her own abilities especially when you aren't present for a school exam or competitive athletic event. Being able to reach into your pocket and touch a crazy lace agate or a piece of flourite can give a worried middle schooler a little confidence and the ability to focus on an important test. For a child experiencing nightmares, placing celestite or selenite under her pillow to ward off bad dreams might make bedtime a little easier.

For all ages, crystals will provide you both a new activity to explore and learn about together. There are stone stores you can visit, books to read and lots of crystals to collect. They vary in price from a dollar to hundreds of dollars but you can have quite a collection for a lot less than it would cost to purchase one video game.

A simple children's book about crystals is called *Crystal Children* by Cooper, Parker and Pylar. It's a book geared to preschool children. They have developed cartoon characters to explain each chakra's purpose. They also show how to use a specific color crystal to help with certain situations or feelings.

Take a field trip to a local store that carries crystals. Check out some books and go with an idea of what type of crystal you might want to purchase ahead of time. Crystal experts say that certain crystals will speak to you, so allow your child to handle them and ask her which ones she likes. Your child might be attracted to a specific color, size or shape. Go with that.

One thing to keep in mind is that if your child is carrying the crystals in her pockets, don't go too big or too small. Crystals, if they are too small, can be easily lost and even if they are only a couple of dollars each, can become expensive to continually replace. If they are too big they can become bulky and uncomfortable to carry around. If you have a child that tends to lose things, like me, then you might look for crystals that can be worn on a string as a necklace or as a keychain to attach to a backpack.

My Crystal Pouch

One way to carry your crystals is in a special pouch.

What you will need:

- Small piece of colorful fabric, about 5 x 10 inches (preferably your child's choice)
- Fabric glue
- Scissors
- String or ribbon about 12 -14 inches long

Fold the fabric in half, length-wise, with the colorful side inside. Line up the top so it is even with the folded half. If you want your bag to be a little smaller, you can cut it on the side to be the size you want. Fold over the top about 1/2 inch on both sides and press with a hot iron (for the adult only). If you don't want to use an iron, then find a heavy book to place onto the fabric for a few minutes to make a creased fold. Glue the sides closed. Once the sides are glued, place your ribbon or string around the entire top fold. Now glue the top fold closed over the ribbon so the ribbon or string is hidden within the fold. Cut the string to the desired length you want in order to be able to tie the top shut. Wait until the glue dries. Flip the whole thing inside out so the colorful side is visible and you should have a great little sack to fill with "magic" crystals.

CHAPTER 24

TEACHING THE IDEA THAT WE ARE ALL CONNECTED

"There are no random acts...We are all connected...You can no more separate one life from another than you can separate a breeze from the wind..."

MITCH ALBOM

The concept that we are all connected as part of a collected consciousness is slowly making its way into marketing campaigns, yoga classes and our belief system. Respect for each other as part of the same human race, while honoring our differences, is a necessary belief for our children to hold dear to their hearts in order to create a harmonious existence with all types of people. It is essential for our children to thrive. The future of our planet depends on us being able to live harmoniously.

If your child is old enough to comprehend this, you can introduce the concept of a "global consciousness." You can explain that there is research being done that shows when people pray or all think of something at the same time, they can effect change out into the world. Believe it or not this includes physical change.

Scientist Bill Tiller is committing himself to testing out this theory. In the book *What The Bleep Do We Know,* by Arntz, Chasse and Vicente, the authors write, "Simply put: Dr. Tiller has four individuals meditate on a simple electronic box to intend something like the pH of water changing one full unit. They ship it off, place it next to some water, and a few months later the pH has changed. There is a less than a thousand to one chance that this change would have occurred naturally, especially given that the change did not occur with the control units." According to Tiller, the change of one full unit in your body is deadly. Therefore it is quite a significant change in physical matter resulting from the consciousness of the group.

The notion that a global consciousness exists is what is behind the concept of world prayer. Many of you might have received emails to participate in one of these worldwide prayer sessions after the 2010 earthquake in Haiti or the 2011 tsunami in Japan.

If prayer is not a part of your family life, you can discuss how people come together in a variety of ways to help each other to effect change. Ask your child to think of some examples. If she can't come up with one you can offer, people working together to clean a park, build a new house or look for a missing pet. Open up a discussion by asking how you cooperate to do something together in your family that maybe just one of you couldn't do alone?

We Are All Connected Activities

Rice Krispie Treats

A fun activity to teach that we are all individuals but are all connected is to make Rice Krispie treats together. If you have an issue with your child eating these sweets for dietary reasons, then you can tell her that you are going to make "decorations."

To make decorations, you can use cookie cutters to create different shapes once the treats have hardened. You can decorate the shapes using other food products such as frosting, gum drops, raisins, straws, pretzels or anything else you can think of that is in your kitchen to create all kinds of fun creations. Use your imagination. Most children usually enjoy the process of cooking more than eating the end product.

Before you begin, show her the Rice Krispies and say, "Imagine that each Rice Krispie is a separate person in the world. The marshmallows can be their thoughts. The butter is the universal energy or glue that allows their thoughts to join together." You can explain that when individuals' thoughts work together as a whole, the whole can create something new and better that didn't exist before. This will become quite apparent once the separate ingredients blend together to form the big squares.

Rice Krispie Treat Recipe

What you will need:

- **3 Tbs butter**
- **1 package of 10-ounce large marshmallows or**
- **4 cups of mini marshmallows**
- **6 cups of Rice Krispies**

In a large saucepan melt the butter over low heat. Add the marshmallows and stir until completely melted. Remove from the heat. Add the Rice Krispies cereal. Stir until well coated. Using a buttered spatula or wax paper evenly press the mixture into a 13x9x2-inch pan coated with cooking spray. Cool. Cut into 2-inch squares or cookie cutter shapes. If eating, these taste best on the same day as baking.

As you are cooking make sure you continue the discussion of how we are all connected. You might point out how many Rice Krispies it takes to fill up six cups. This can lead to how many people there are in your family, your town and the world. Discuss how each ingredient is important to creating the recipe correctly and getting the end result you want. Discuss with your older children how individual actions affects others in the world like recycling their water bottles. Have them try to think of individuals who have made life-changing impacts on our lives like inventors. This might be hard for younger children to understand but listening to the conversation will plant the seed of understanding for later on.

Family Puzzles

Doing a large puzzle together as a family teaches cooperation and the importance of each piece contributing to the whole. If you have ever put together a puzzle, then you might remember searching to find the one missing piece in order for it to be complete. This is a concrete example of how every individual matters, no matter how small.

Set up an area where the puzzle can stay undisturbed so you can work on it over time if need be. Try, if possible, to work together since this will provide a great opportunity for conversation.

What you will need:

- **A large puzzle with many pieces that is appropriate for your age children**

If this is a puzzle that takes several days or weeks to do then I suggest you use puzzle glue on it once you complete it. This will give you something to look back at and see how you all worked together cooperatively as a team to make something together. There might be many times when you need to glance at it for encouragement when things aren't running so harmoniously!

Creating a Family Mural

What you will need:

- A large piece of drawing paper off an art roll (You can purchase rolls of drawing paper at a craft store.) or
- The back of wrapping paper, the side that isn't printed on or individual construction paper
- Drawing utensils such as markers, paints, colored pencils, crayons
- Glue
- Scissors

A family mural is a great opportunity for you to create something as a family. Through the process you can show how each of you contributes to creating the whole. You can do this in a couple of ways and with a variety of materials depending on the age and patience of your children.

One way is to offer each child her own piece of paper and art material such as markers, crayons and paints. Before beginning, you might discuss a topic or theme that you want to create for your mural. Some ideas are happy memories, favorite places, favorite things to do together, and what makes each unique in the family. Once each child is finished with her drawing, you can then glue her piece of paper onto a larger one. You can also just tape the individual sheets together.

You can also use one large piece of paper, as suggested above, that you might use from a paper roll and have the children work simultaneously. This will require a lot more family cooperation.

Family Mosaic

What you will need:

- **Mosaic tiles along with the appropriate adhesive. (You can purchase these at a craft store or where tiles are sold.)**
- **A wooden board to which the mosaics will adhere. (I suggest a standard size that will fit into a frame in case you choose to frame your end product.)**
- **Markers or colored pencils**

This project is one that will challenge your older children (middle school age). It will require patience, cooperation and fine motor control.

To begin, you will need to come up with a concept of what you want to create. Once you have the idea, assign each child her part in the project. For example, maybe you decide to make a picture of your family home. You can assign each child a portion of the house to work on. For example, one works on the windows, another the roof and another the outline. Remind each that her role is essential to creating the whole picture and that without her contribution the picture wouldn't be complete.

Draw onto the board what you want to create. Using the markers, fill in the design with colors you want to use for the mosaics. This will offer a visual clue for each child. Allow each child the opportunity for her individual creative expression.

Working on any family project together will offer many rewards. It will reaffirm to each child that she is a unique individual with significant impact on the whole. It will inevitably also offer each child an opportunity to work on the social skills of patience, negotiation and cooperation while providing an amazing opportunity for imagination and creativity to flourish.

CHAPTER 25

CAUSE AND EFFECT

"Shallow men believe in luck, believe in circumstances...
Strong men believe in cause and effect."
RALPH WALDO EMERSON

Building on the concepts of karma and that we are all connected is the principle of cause and effect. For older children, you might bring up a discussion about the "butterfly effect" principle. The phrase refers to the idea that the flapping of a butterfly's wings on one side of the world might create small changes in the atmosphere that would ultimately effect weather conditions on the opposite side of the world. From a human perspective, this theory suggests that even the smallest of actions may have huge consequences on the greater whole.

This is an empowering concept for a child to ponder, especially a child who is on the verge of being able to make her own decisions. Children, by nature, are egocentric. Infants are born this way as a means of survival. As our children grow older we hope as parents to teach them responsibility for themselves and consideration for others. They may first begin to learn this at around age two when they see something they want and grab it from another child and that child reacts by screaming. They see how their behavior, grabbing

PARENTING WITH AWARENESS

the toy, specifically caused the response of the other child namely their crying.

As parents, it is our responsibility to teach our children the effects of their behavior. We offer parental promptings like, "That wasn't nice," or "Say you are sorry," or "You have to share," in an attempt to teach appropriate social skills and manners. The goal is to instill the awareness that their behavior affects others so that they act appropriately with the concern for others in mind.

What is nice about children being aware of the butterfly effect principle, whether it is true or just a theory, is that the idea will empower them. From a young age they will believe they can make a difference through their actions. If children are taught that whatever they do or think has an impact out in the world, then they will be encouraged to participate and to act on their beliefs. It's the opposite of how most of us were raised with the idea that, "I am just one person. What can I do to make a difference?" As adults we often wrestle with a sense of helplessness when confronted with huge issues like global warming, world hunger or the economy. We feel powerless, so we end up doing nothing. This only reinforces the victim mentality. Teaching children from a young age that their contribution effects the whole, will plant the seed for them to always act from a global consciousness.

There are many examples throughout history where one man's behavior impacted an entire society or even the world. Two examples are the positive impact of the pure wisdom taught by Buddha to the horrific evil inflicted by Adolph Hitler. Individuals can and do make a difference. You may not recognize the name Richard Colvin Reid but if you travel, he has impacted your life. He is commonly known as the "Shoe Bomber." On December 22, 2001, he boarded American Airlines Flight 63 from Paris to Miami, wearing his special shoes packed with plastic explosives, in their hollowed-out bottoms, in an attempt

278

to blow up the plane. Because of him, everyone now has to go through the inconvenience of taking off their shoes to go through airport security. The lasting effects of his actions continues to cause millions to be inconvenienced. With the butterfly effect in mind, set the example for your child that one individual can make a difference. Show her that even if you can't see the result immediately, her actions might make an enormous difference in the future.

The idea of cause and effect can be difficult for a child to believe in especially when the ramifications of what they do now seem to be long off in the distant future. It's relatively easy to show a toddler that her behavior of biting her friend caused him to cry. It's a lot harder to prove to a child in middle school that the track of course work she chooses now will effect the type of college that will accept her when she graduates high school in six years. Or, how do you convince a teenager that inappropriate pictures placed on Facebook now could effect a job position fifteen years in the future? Possessing the awareness of cause and effect is essential in making good choices for oneself. It's a concept worth practicing.

Below are some concrete ways to begin to teach cause and effect.

Cause and Effect Game

What you will need:

- **A set of dominoes**

Dominoes offer a visual way of expressing cause and effect. They will show how the smallest action can have a big impact.

Did you know according to the *Guinness Book of Records*, that the greatest number of dominoes set up single-handed and toppled is 303,621 out of 303,628 by Ma Li Hua (China) at Singapore Expo Hall, Singapore on August 18, 2003? You won't need to set up nearly that many to get your point across!

Most toy stores sell dominoes fairly inexpensively. However, if you don't want to buy them, you can create a similar visual with empty juice boxes or rectangular wooden blocks. You won't be able to set up as an elaborate track but for little hands these may be easier to manipulate.

Make sure you place your dominoes or boxes equal distance apart so that when one is toppled (*the cause*) it will bump into the next one and knock it over (*the effect*). You can try to impact the dominoes through a variety of ways. First, have your child blow on them and see how many topple over. Next, you can have her use her pinky finger, a toe, maybe a feather or a stick. Play around with how you start the sequence of falling to begin. Another thing to consider is if your course is straight or if it takes twists and turns like life does. You can let your child configure the design. This will offer an opportunity for creativity. This activity also will teach eye-hand coordination, visual discrimination, counting, imagination and planning skills. If you have a pet, make sure it is not around. It would be quite upsetting to spend a long time setting up your track only to have the dog run in and knock it over! Then it would also teach forgiveness.

Kaleidoscopes

I absolutely love kaleidoscopes for their ability to continuously create simple beauty with no two designs exactly the same. David Brewster, a Scottish scientist invented the kaleidoscope in 1816. He named his invention after the Greek words, *kalos* or beautiful, *eidos* or form, and *scopos* or watcher. So kaleidoscope means the beautiful form watcher.

Modern-day kaleidoscopes can be made from many materials including brass, wood and stone. They can be quite costly, selling for hundreds of dollars. Some of the most beautiful are ones whose object chamber is filled with a liquid, often an oil. This allows the objects to float through the chamber with the slightest of movement. Kaleidoscopes are most often sold in galleries and online. If you can't afford one, perhaps you can visit a local gallery to show your child several types of kaleidoscopes.

Toy kaleidoscopes can be found online and are fairly inexpensive. Kaleidoscopes offer the ability to teach children in a very visual way the universal concepts of cause and effect and the idea that we are all connected. It will be quite easy for your child to see that any movement of the kaleidoscope has a specific impact in changing the interior design.

The universal principle that we are all separate and unique human beings but also all connected and part of a whole can be overwhelming to comprehend and believe even for the adult mind. The kaleidoscope is able to visually explain this. Ask your child to hold the kaleidoscope still and have her describe to you what she sees. She should see many separate colored items. Then have her slowly move the kaleidoscope. As she is doing this, have her describe to you how what she sees has changed. Explain to her that the design she now sees is made up of all of the same smaller pieces. You can ask her to look for a specific thing in the kaleidoscope such as a blue bead and ask her to see where it ends up in the design each time she moves it. Talk about how the big design needs each of the smaller pieces in order to create itself.

You can explain that our planet Earth reacts in a similar way. Explain how we may all live separately but what one person does can affect many people. Ask her to think of some examples of how one person can affect others. Some suggestions to begin the discussion are:

"How does an individual affect a team sport like soccer?"

"What happens if one of the players is tired and doesn't try her best?"

"What happens in school if one child behaves badly in class?"

After discussing these concrete examples, you can ask her something more abstract like:

"How does her mood affect those around her?"

"How is she affected by someone else's mood?"

For older children you can then move on to more global issues like:

"What would happen if a chemical company poured their waste into the ocean?"

"What would happen if a president of a country said that girls couldn't go to school?"

Another universal principle that the kaleidoscope is able to visually teach is that nothing in the universe is permanent. Have your child hold the kaleidoscope still. Now, have her move it ever so slightly. How did the design change? It will be quite apparent that even the slightest movement can totally set in motion the entire pattern to change. This is similar to the butterfly effect we discussed above. Explain that everything is always changing, in us, and all around us. Ask her to describe things she notices that change. You can start the conversation with a simple example such as the weather. Then see what she comes up with since it will give you insight into her ideas.

Introducing the idea that everything changes at a young age will help your child to be flexible in her beliefs and attitudes. It will also help her to understand that she has to be adaptable. Situations like divorce, joblessness, moving, birth of a new sibling and even death are all life-challenging events that occur because of change. Being aware that change is part of life will prepare her for when she has to experience a life-changing event in the future. A Buddhist sutra states, "Unceasing change turns the wheel of life, and so reality is shown in all its many forms. Dwell peacefully as change itself liberates all suffering sentient beings and brings them great joy."

The idea that we are all connected and what one does has an impact on others are two essential messages we need to teach our children if we are going to continue to thrive as humans on this planet. This is not an easy task when our world leaders lie; our business moguls steal; and our sport idols are motivated to play from greed. As adults, we become angry when leaders we trusted betray us. As a society, we are running out of heroes for our children to look up to. How do we inspire and motivate our children in things we can no longer believe as absolute truths?

However, there is hope. According to numerology, under the power of the "two energy" which supports peace and co-operation, our planetary consciousness is now beginning to change, beginning with the turn of the century. Our minds are now opening to the idea of global cooperation. People are now beginning to stand up against the avaricious behavior that has motivated so many in power for way too long. This is a very different mentality than the self-centered attitude that persisted throughout the 1900s.

In the future, as natural resources dwindle, sharing will not be just an admirable attribute, but a necessity. Issues such as global warming, terrorism and the ailing world economy won't just be ideas that liberal politicians exploit as platforms for elections. These issues and others will need to be addressed by all, if we are going to continue to thrive as a race and our planet continue to exist. We need to teach our children, when they are young, that the old mentality to view everyone else as an obstacle or competitor is no longer necessary. We need to believe we can create a society where by working together, sharing our resources and living in peace we can all realize our individual goals.

As a people, maybe we need to look back to gain the insight necessary to move forward. A first step is to look at these ancient wisdoms with new belief and optimism. Our ancestors possessed essential knowledge that unfortunately was lost behind our fixated mindset: to build, acquire and develop at all costs. This mentality led us into the industrial revolution and the technical advancements resulting in the incredible growth we have experienced on our planet over the last 200 years. Some inventions have been beneficial and life changing, such as advanced medical procedures and medications that now prolong our lives. Others have led to devastating consequences resulting in nuclear destruction, permanent damage to our environment; the economic collapse of many governments and useless wars. All have changed the way we currently exist and experience life on our planet. As always everything happens for a reason.

For over 3,200 years, since God gave Moses the Bible, there has been the belief that the Bible held a secret encoded message for mankind about our destiny that would be revealed in the "End of Days." Since then, numerous geniuses have tried to uncover its hidden truths to gain insight about where we are headed. As we now approach December 2012, the end of the Hebrew and Mayan calendars, many believe we are near the End of Days. Although we have made many devastating mistakes in our advancement process, it is precisely through our understanding of technology and the invention of the computer that has allowed us access to information encoded in the Bible.

Eliyahu Rips, an Israeli mathematician, designed a computer program he claims is able to decipher or unlock a hidden code within the Bible. He did this by removing all the punctuation to create one long word approximately 300,000 letters long. Michael Drosnin, a journalist and author, documented what Rips discovered in his books, *The Bible Code I, II and III*. Initially he was suspicious of the validity of the code. However, every time the code has been put to the test, by independent mathematicians, it has proven to be valid. The code has foretold major historical events including the assassination of Prime Minister Yitzhak Rabin, the Tsunami in Asia, hurricane Katrina, 911 and the election of Barack Obama before he was considered a candidate. However, the most incessant message is that no matter what has been written, we always have the power to change it. From this, one can conclude that how our destiny will unfold as the human race on this planet is ultimately up to us.

Recent events such as the capture and killing of world terrorists might have averted a global conflict. Protesters fighting against the inequalities in our current economic system might initiate a political change. We will never know exactly how any single event or action determines the future, but it inevitably does. As individuals we always have the power within us to change the events of our lives. Collectively, we have the power to change the world we live in. Steven Jobs wrote, "The people who are crazy enough to think they can change the world are the ones who do."

As a parent, you have that extraordinary power to implement change. You can make a conscientious decision to break from the current style of parenting which is ego driven based in a competitive mentally. Begin to instill in your child the need to live from a sense of awareness that includes a global consciousness. I encourage you to focus on what your child can contribute instead of what she can achieve. Parent with the priority to raise an enlightened child inspired to become an empowered adult. Nurture her from a sense of respect. Cherish your child's individual soul by honoring her unique life to unfold, at its own pace, and bloom in its own way.

I implore you to make a commitment to trust. Trust in your parental instincts, trust the universe for the gifts it has to assist you and most importantly, trust your child to be guided by her innate wisdom and passions. Within each of us is the seed to become the best that we can be. This seed, within your child, needs your unconditional love, patience, and unconditional acceptance, to germinate and bloom to its full potential. These are the essential gifts you can offer your child, allowing her to become her best self. The only self she can be.

Index of Activities:

Chapter 23: Crystals and the Power of Magic Stones
Crystal Pouch

Chapter 24: Teaching the Idea that We are All Connected
Rice Krispie Treats
Family Puzzle Making
Family Mural
Family Mosaic

Chapter 25: Cause and Effect
Dominoes
Exploring kaleidoscopes

To view activities and other book information go to
parentingwithawareness.net

BIBLIOGRAPHY

Arntz, W, Chase, B, & Vincente, M. *What the Bleep Do We Know.* Deerfield Beach, FL: Health Communications, Inc., 2005.

Braden, G. *Fractal Time.* Carlsbad, CA: Hay House, 2009.

Chopra, D. *Power Freedom Grace.* San Rafael, CA: Amber Allen Publishing, 2006.

Coelho, P. *Eleven Minutes.* New York, NY: Harper Colllins, 2000.

Drosnin, M. *Bible Code II.* New York, NY: Penguin Books. 2002.

Drosnin, M. *Bible Code III Saving the World?* New York, NY: Worldmedia, 2010.

Elkind, D. *The Hurried Child.* Cambridge, MA: Da Capo Books, 1981.

Elkind, D. *The Power of Play.* Philadeplhia, PA: DA Capo Press, 2007.

Emoto, M. *The Secret Life Of Water.* Hillsboro, OR: Beyond Words Publishing, 2005.

Gladwell, M. *Outliers.* New York, NY: Little Brown and CO, 2008.

Hairfield, L. S. *The Twelve Sacred Principles of Karma.* Breinigsville, PA, 2010.

Hall, K. *Aspire.* New York, NY: HarperCollins, 2010.

Hardie, T. *Tatiania's Book of Numerology.* Philadephia, PA: Quadrille Publishers, 2000.

Jordan, J. *Numerology The Romance in Your Name.* Camarillo, CA: JF Rowney Press, 1965.

Katie, B. *Loving What Is.* New York, NY: Three Rivers Press, 2002.

Kornfield, J. *The Art Of Forgiveness, Loving Kindness and Peace.* New York, NY, 2002.

Lagerquist, K., & Lenard, L. *The Colplete idiot's Guuide to Numerology.* Indianapolis, IN: Amaranth Illuminare, 2004.

Mulford, P. *Thoughts Are Things.* New York, NY: Barnes and Noble, 2007.

Murphy, J. *The Power of Your Subconscious Mind.* Lexington, KY: SoHo Books, 2010.

Pasek-Hirsh, K. P, Golinkoff Michnick, R. P, & Eyer, D. P. *Einstein Never Used Flashcards.* Emmaus, PA: Rodale, 2003.

Permutt, P. *The Crystal Healer.* New York, NY: CICO Books, 2007.

Ruiz, D. M., *The Four Agreements.* San Rafael, CA: Amber Allen Publishing, 1997.

Shafir, R. *The Zen Of Listening.* Wheaton, Illinois: Quest Books, 2000.

Silverstein, S. *The Giving Tree.* New York, NY: Harper Collins, 1964.

Suess, D. *My Many Colored Days.* New York, NY: Random House, 1996.

Virtue, D. & Brown, L. *Angel Numbers.* Carlsbad, CA: Hay House, 2005.

Virtue, D. & Virtue, G. *Angel Words.* Carlsbad, CA, USA: Hay House, 2010.

Warner, J. *Perfect Madness.* New York, NY: Penguin Group, 2005.

Wauters, A. *The Book of Chakras.* Hauppage, NY: Quarto Books, 2002.

Williamson, M. *A Return To Love.* New York, NY: Harper Collins, 1992.

Marcie's dynamic personality has been educating parents and enchanting children in a variety of capacities for the past 30 years including the unique Marcie and Me educational play program she founded. Her parenting expertise is derived from the thousands of families she has worked with as well as raising her two adult sons and three stepchildren.

As a teen, Marcie channeled her passion and drive into gymnastics earning her several National Titles and two Gold Medals at the 1977 Maccabiah games in Israel.

She attended Clark University earning degrees in special education and psychology and went on to pursue her graduate studies in early education at Tufts University and Wheelock College.

Marcie currently teaches in her Marcie and Me play program in Westwood, Massachusetts where she resides with her husband. She is an educational speaker, parent coach and an award-winning photographer.

To schedule a Book Presentation or Parenting Workshop, please contact Marcie at **parentingwithawareness.net**